EYE ON
ART

Graphic Design
Putting Art and Words Together

By Donna Reynolds

Portions of this book originally appeared in *Graphic Design* by Stuart A. Kallen.

LUCENT
PRESS

Published in 2018 by
Lucent Press, an Imprint of Greenhaven Publishing, LLC
353 3rd Avenue
Suite 255
New York, NY 10010

Designer: Seth Hughes
Editor: Jennifer Lombardo

Cataloging-in-Publication Data

Names: Reynolds, Donna.
Title: Graphic design: putting Art and words together / Donna Reynolds.
Description: New York : Lucent Press, 2018. | Series: Eye on art | Includes index.
Identifiers: ISBN 9781534560994 (library bound) | ISBN 9781534561007 (ebook)
Subjects: LCSH: Graphic arts–Juvenile literature.
Classification: LCC NC997.R49 2018 | DDC 740–dc23

Printed in the United States of America

CPSIA compliance information: Batch #BS17KL: For further information contact Greenhaven Publishing LLC, New York, New York at 1-844-317-7404.

Please visit our website, www.greenhavenpublishing.com. For a free color catalog of all our high-quality books, call toll free 1-844-317-7404 or fax 1-844-317-7405.

Contents

Foreword

When many people think of art, the first things that come to mind may be paintings, drawings, sculptures, or even pictures created entirely with a computer. However, people have been applying artistic elements to almost every aspect of life for thousands of years. Human beings love beautiful things, and they seek beauty in unlikely places. Buildings, clothes, furniture, and many other things we use every day can all have an artistic aspect to them.

Attempts to define art have frequently fallen short. Merriam-Webster defines art as "something that is created with imagination and skill and that is beautiful or that expresses important ideas or feelings." However, almost no one refers to the dictionary definition when attempting to decide whether or not something can be considered art. They rely on their intuition, which leaves much room for debate between competing opinions. What one person views as beautiful, another may see as ugly. An idea that an artist feels it is important to express may hit home with some people and be dismissed by others. Some people believe that art should always be beautiful, while others feel that art should be unsettling enough to pull people out of their comfort zone. With all of these contradictory views, it is no wonder that the question of what is art is so often disputed.

This series aims to introduce readers to some of the more unconventional and controversial art forms, such as anime, fashion design, and graffiti. Debate on these topics has often been heated, with some people firmly declaring that they are art and others declaring just as firmly that they are not. Each book in the series discusses the history of a particular art form, the ways it is created, and the reasons why it is considered artistic. Learning more about these topics helps young adults recognize the art that is all around them as well as form their own opinions about this complex subject.

Quotes by experts in various art fields enhance the engaging text. All quotes are cited so readers can trace them back to their original source, giving them a starting point for further research. A list of recommended books and websites also allows young adults to delve deeper into related subjects. Full-color photographs give vivid examples of the artistic works being described in the books so readers can visualize the terms they are learning.

Through this series, young adults gain a better understanding of a variety of popular art forms. They also develop a deeper appreciation for the artistry that is inherent in the things they see and use every day.

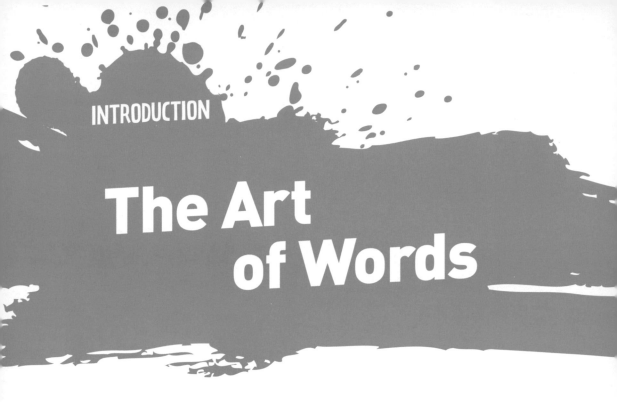

The Art of Words

Graphic design is everywhere in today's society, to such an extent that many people no longer consciously notice it. Many business logos, T-shirt designs, posters, and other everyday items carry examples of graphic design. Some designs are intended to sell products; others are done as a way for artists to communicate a particular message. Some people feel that graphic design should not be considered art, but others believe the skill and time required to create beautiful, eye-catching designs qualifies graphic designers as artists.

In its earliest days, graphic art was based on mixing art, craft, business, science, technology, and language. In the 15th century, the science of ink and paper production was blended with the technology of the printing press. This created the business of book production, in which graphic artists combined art and language. In the 19th century, science and technology led to the invention of the lithographic press, the camera, and the photogravure reproduction process. These developments created a mass-media revolution that was driven by eye-catching graphic designs. Today, designers continue to rely on art, craft, business, science, technology, and language to create cutting-edge websites, as well as more traditional forms of graphic design.

The Debate Over Graphic Design

However artful their products may be, graphic designers are not considered fine artists such as painters and sculptors. Because most graphic art relies on words and text as well as pictures and illustrations, graphic designs are generally considered forms of communication rather than art. While fine artists often rely on obscure symbolism that can be interpreted in numerous ways, it is generally required that graphic artists communicate messages clearly so they can be understood by nearly everyone.

That is not to say that the artistic aspect cannot be emphasized in graphic design. In fact, some of the great art movements of the past century, such as modernism, art deco, and cubism, found their way into graphic arts. By incorporating these styles into their work, graphic artists rejected the division between fine art and commercial art. In doing so, they created a visual poetry that inventively combines words and images into clever and aesthetically pleasing messages. Like any good art, quality graphic arts can fuel the imagination.

While the majority of graphic art is used for mundane communications, lasting designs have become part of the social fabric. For example, the Coca-Cola logo is instantly recognized in nearly every country on Earth. Logos for other companies, such as Apple, Mercedes Benz, and McDonald's, are similarly well-known.

Painters such as Leonardo da Vinci might have incorporated dozens of symbols into a single painting that viewers could debate for centuries, but Coca-Cola wants to sell its product to people in America, Armenia, and Afghanistan. A simple piece of graphic art has allowed them to communicate this message to billions of people speaking thousands of languages in hundreds of countries throughout the world.

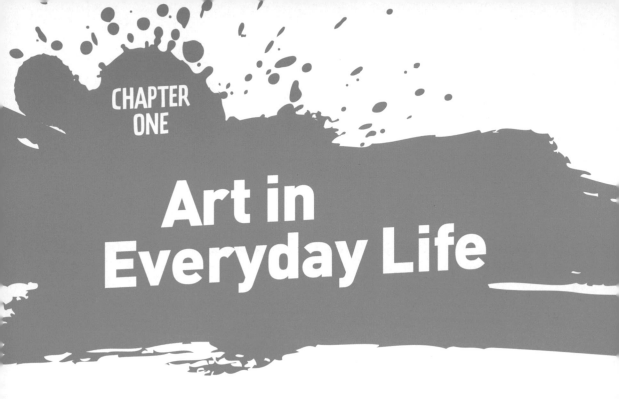

CHAPTER ONE

Art in Everyday Life

The challenge graphic designers take on with their work is how to communicate quickly, clearly, and effectively. Their work must send a message that can be understood by the majority of people who see it. In addition to using text, graphic designers can achieve this goal by using picture images called pictographs or pictograms. These let them communicate even with people who do not speak the same language. Pictograms are simply pictures of the thing they represent; for instance, a picture of a bicycle communicates the idea of a bicycle.

Pictograms, either alone or in different combinations, can be used as ideograms, which represent more complex ideas. Ideograms generally have meaning because society has agreed on that meaning. For example, the "power" button on many electronic devices is a semicircle partially bisected by a vertical line segment. This comes from the binary system of 1s and 0s that computers use, where a 1 (the line) represents "on" and a 0 (the circle) represents "off." Older devices had switches with a line on one side and a circle on the other. As electronics advanced and a single power button was created, the line and circle were combined. Most people do not know where the design came from, but they all recognize it and know what the button will do when they see it.

No matter what language they speak, when people see this symbol, they understand that it indicates the power button on an electronic device.

Of course, the best-designed message is no use if people never see it. This is why graphic artists must also make sure their design is eye-catching. They often do this using various colors, textures, shapes, and fonts, arranged in ways that are striking enough to draw the eye.

The composition of a design— the way it is put together—may be determined by what is around it as well as the information the designer is trying to convey. For instance, although bright colors are generally eye-catching, a black and white poster may stand out more or look more pleasing on a brightly colored wall than a colorful poster would. Designers can change the brightness (the lightness or darkness of something), saturation (the dullness or intensity of a color), weight (how thick a line or the letters in a font are), and other details to make their designs stand out. Using different combinations of design elements can allow two designers to present the same information in very different ways. For instance, a black-and-white picture often makes people think of class and sophistication, while red and black often makes them think of danger. Changing just one color can give an image an entirely different mental association.

Using Pictures to Convey Meaning

Symbols are a basic unit of visual communication, but they can be used to convey complex words, concepts, ideas, and actions. Therefore, a variety of symbols has been developed that express ideas, concepts, words, or phrases. Pictograms, ideograms, and logograms have been common throughout the development of human civilization and remain so today.

Pictograms represent objects and were first drawn on cave walls in Africa and Europe more than 30,000 years ago. The simple symbols that have survived represent bison, deer, birds, the sun, and other things that were important to the people of that time. Drawings also include stick figures that symbolize people, villages, and hunters holding shields and spears. Anthropologists speculate that these early graphic communications were either used as symbols in religious rites or simply as a way to leave a message to those who followed. Whatever their exact purpose, the images in the prehistoric pictograms are still understood by people 300 centuries after they were drawn.

Ideograms generally represent more complex concepts. The most common ideograms are Arabic numerals. For example, the numeral 5 represents the idea of five units and can be used to quantify anything from apples to asteroids.

One popular ideogram, the heart symbol (♥), stands for the complex concept of love. In the world of advertising, the ideogram "I ♥ NY" ("I love New York"), created by legendary graphic designer Milton Glaser, was a breakthrough that has been imitated countless times. Such simple designs have become critical in advertising at a time when many cities and corporations are marketing themselves to people all over the world.

While ideograms symbolize concepts, logograms represent words or phrases. A simple logogram, the ampersand (&), is the sign that represents the word " and." In more complex forms, the written Chinese language is composed of 50,000 characters, some of which evolved over time from pictograms into logograms and ideograms. In Chinese writing, a pictogram shaped like a crescent moon changed to become a symbol that represents the word "moon." Ideograms in the shape of a T or inverted T are used to express the words "above" or "below." Logograms are drawn when entire phrases need to be expressed. Taken together, Chinese characters are highly stylized pictures that express words, phrases, ideas, feelings, colors, actions, sizes, and types of objects.

love

trust

賀　　　心　　　謝

celebrate　　　heart　　　thank

The written Chinese language is made up of symbols that express ideas.

The Design of the Dollar Bill

In the United States, the $1 bill is packed with pictograms and ideograms. However, the symbols on it are either ignored or misunderstood by many Americans.

One of the most enduring symbols on the dollar is the Great Seal of the United States. The symbol's creation was decreed by the Continental Congress on July 4, 1776, the same day that the Declaration of Independence was signed. However, it took nearly six years and numerous revisions by graphic artists before the symbol was adopted.

The meaning of the Great Seal has been debated for more than two centuries since Benjamin Franklin, John Adams, and Thomas Jefferson first proposed the design.

The front of the Great Seal shows ideograms of an American eagle, a shield, an olive branch, and 13 arrows. The eagle represents the idea of freedom, the shield stands for the concept of strength, and the arrows are symbolic of the 13 original colonies. The arrows and the olive branch also represent war and peace. The back of the Great Seal, on the left side of the dollar, shows an unfinished or uncapped pyramid. Hovering above the symbol is the capstone, which, if lowered, would complete the pyramid. Inside the capstone is an eye, called the Eye of Providence, surrounded by rays of light. The U.S. Treasury Department provides the official meaning of the symbols: "The unfinished pyramid means that the United States will always grow, improve and build ... [The] 'All-Seeing Eye' located above the pyramid suggests the importance of divine guidance in favor of the American cause."[1]

The pictures on the $1 bill have symbolic meaning related to the United States.

While few people bother to look closely at their money as they spend it, these ideograms have created controversy over the centuries. Some have concluded that the symbols are occult icons that represent an ancient secret society called the Freemasons. The symbols are sometimes interpreted to mean that the Founding Fathers were Freemasons who wanted to impose a tyrannical new world order on the people of the United States. Although modern Freemasons deny this rumor, it has been repeated continually for centuries and remains a featured topic on several conspiracy websites.

Symbols of Power

The debate over the symbols on the dollar bill prove how powerful graphic designs can be. This was understood by medieval artists who created designs called coats of arms to represent knights, nobles, and influential families. The symbols used on these complex graphic creations were meant to inspire fear, respect, and awe in the people who viewed them.

In modern times, coats of arms are seen on product logos, dinnerware, and the letterheads of colleges and universities. Even fictional places, such as Hogwarts School of Witchcraft and Wizardry from the Harry Potter series, can have a coat of arms. However, in centuries past, a coat of arms was a highly respected symbol that was passed from father to eldest son. The uses of the coat of arms were governed by strict laws.

The word "heraldry" came into use in the 12th century to define the art of creating a coat of arms. Those who practiced heraldry originally designed

NOVA SCOTIA

1867

PRINCE EDWARD ISL.

1873

Cities, states, and other places can create their own coat of arms. Shown here are the coats of arms of three Canadian provinces.

coats of arms to be displayed on helmets, chest armor, or shields of knights. A coat of arms would identify a knight when he participated in battles. A knight would also display the symbols on armor and banners when competing in tournaments that featured mock combat between opponents.

In these tournaments, a well-known coat of arms was like an advertisement for the bearer. It informed spectators of the knight's character, qualifications, and lineage. Everything on the coat of arms was symbolic; the pictures were not just for decoration.

The shield was the central element on the coat of arms and resembled metal shields used for protection in battle. A shield may contain images called charges, such as the traditional lion or a lily flower design called a fleur-de-lis. Other charges included a chevron (v-shaped line) for protection, a crown designating royal authority, or a hydra (a dragon with seven heads), which meant the bearer had conquered a very

The Rise of Graphic Design

In the early 20th century, improved methods of production and communication created a culture increasingly based on consumerism. This required a growing number of skilled graphic artists to work for printers and publishers, as British design historian Jeremy Aynsley explained in *A Century of Graphic Design*:

Graphic design was a new profession for a new century. Its emergence was underpinned by major technological changes ... For the modern communications system to emerge an infrastructure of mechanized printing, ink and paper manufacture and specialist machinery for folding, binding and stapling was necessary. This was prompted by a huge change in the pattern of life of urban populations ... The migration of people to towns and cities to find industrialized work, the growth of railway networks and the steady increase in the mass market for consumer goods were linked to other important changes. Modern communications became dependent on reproduction, at first through print and later in the century through radio, television and film. Books, magazines, posters and advertisements began to be produced on an unprecedented scale, for instruction, education and entertainment. This led ... to the concentration of large-scale printing houses in cities.

The responsibility to train young workers for the graphic trades and industries had previously belonged to the guilds, but now trade schools and colleges of art and design took on the task ... Matters of taste and aesthetics were taught alongside technical skills. An understanding of [decoration] was considered fundamental to all branches of design and the best way to reform taste.[1]

1. Jeremy Aynsley, *A Century of Graphic Design*. Hauppauge, NY: Barron's Educational Series, 2001, p. 14.

powerful enemy. Background colors on the shield also had specific meanings. Blue was symbolic of truth and loyalty. Gold spoke of generosity, and red informed viewers that the knight was a warrior with great military strength. Other elements of the coat of arms also had specific meanings related to the knight's family heritage.

Coats of arms still displayed by the Vatican and European nobles can be traced back 800 years or more. The Japanese equivalent, called *kamon*, have been used by some families for more than 13 centuries. Perhaps one of the most famous Japanese *kamon*, the Mitsubishi logo represented by three diamonds, has its roots in an ancient family of warriors called the Tosa clan. Another coat of arms associated with automobiles may be found on Porsches. This badge is the coat of arms of the city of Stuttgart, where the cars are made. The rearing horse in the center of the shield honors the ancient horse-breeding farm where the Porsche factory was built. The antlers and red and black stripes are taken from the coat of arms representing the kingdom of Württemberg, now part of Germany, where Stuttgart is located.

Recognizable Logos

Today, logos are pasted on nearly everything in a modern home, including baby toys, T-shirts, televisions, and kitchen appliances. Designer logos are considered to add value to a product; someone may pay many times more for a purse with Louis Vuitton's signature LV logo on it than for a plain purse.

Modern logos have their roots in trademarks, which are any marks or signs on a product that identify its origin. These marks first appeared on bricks and roof tiles in Mesopotamia and Egypt more than 3,000 years ago. During the days of ancient Rome, more than 2,000 years ago, trademarks on bricks contained unusual symbols that identified the county where the bricks were made, the manufacturer's name, the estate where the clay was found, the building contractor, and even the name of the emperor. These trademarks were probably created for tax purposes—they listed everyone who profited from the production of the brick. However, they have left historians with an interesting record of Roman life. For example, the prevalence of female names on the trademarks indicates that women were operating heavy construction businesses in ancient times.

In later centuries, trademarks appeared on tiles, pottery, and hand-carved building stones. After the invention of the printing press in the 15th century, publishers began putting their personal symbols, called colophons, on their books. Because many books were considered works of art in the mid-1400s, colophons began as a way for a printer to sign the work, much as an artist would sign a painting. Within a century, colophons were printed or hand stamped in color on nearly every book.

As the centuries passed, trademarks became less complicated and mysterious. By the late 19th century, there was a growing number of manufacturers, and each was striving to distinguish itself in the marketplace. Trademark designers were faced with the task of conveying the type of product, the producer, and the nature of the business in the shortest way possible. To do so, they designed trademarks, also called logos, which would be used on labels, bottles, letterheads, advertisements, and signs. Today, "trademark" is generally used as a legal term; a company can trademark its logo so no one else can use it or anything that looks too much like it.

By the 20th century, it was an established notion that any business hoping for lasting success needed a memorable logo. In *Seven Designers Look at Trademark Design*, Austrian graphic artist Herbert Bayer explained the qualities of a good logo:

> The aim of [the logo] ... is to catch attention, *to create* interest, *to be pleasing and attractive for* aesthetic *and* psychological *reasons, to* persuade *the observer to buy. In achieving this, the idea of consciously or subconsciously remembering the ... message is of greatest importance. Here is where a well conceived trademark properly used will function best. A good mark is a visual shortcut with the special property of remaining recognized after it has once made a place for itself in the world of symbols.*[2]

The Art of Logo Design

Many hours of work go into creating a logo that is eye-catching and easily recognizable. Often there is some kind of symbolism in logos, but few people think about what that symbolism might be. For instance, the Amazon logo features a yellow arrow underneath the word, pointing from the first "a" to the "z." This indicates that the company sells everything from A to Z. Amazon also calls it a smile, which symbolizes customer satisfaction. This "hidden" meaning is easy to see, but some logos require a longer look to see their symbolic meaning. For instance, the logo of Beats headphones appears at first glance to be simply a lowercase "b" inside a circle, but upon closer inspection, it also looks like a person wearing a pair of Beats headphones.

Some logos are simple enough to be understood at first glance, but even that simplicity requires a lot of thought by a designer. For example, the logo of Apple computers—an apple with a bite taken out of it—obviously represents the name of the company. However, the bite in the apple was added because without it, it could too easily be confused with a cherry. The designers needed to make sure the logo would not cause confusion; everyone looking at it needed to understand immediately that they were seeing an apple.

The logo of Beats headphones was designed to have a double meaning.

A Graphic Arts Pioneer

With so much importance attached to a relatively simple piece of graphics, perhaps it is not surprising that some of the most talented designers were hired by companies to create corporate artwork. Some of these artists designed logos and labels, while others expanded their horizons to create furniture, wallpaper, textiles, and architectural designs. German graphic artist Peter Behrens produced it all.

Behrens studied painting as a young man, but by 1900, he became interested in the designs of the arts and crafts movement. Based in Great Britain, proponents of the arts and crafts style stood in opposition to the cheap, mass-produced goods of the Victorian era. The founders of the movement valued styles based on beautiful designs that could be created by skilled craftspeople, who were increasingly unemployed during the factory era. As movement founder William Morris stated, arts and crafts products were created "for the people and by the people, and a source of pleasure to the maker and the user."[3]

Inspired by Morris's words, Behrens designed a villa in Darmstadt in 1901 based on the arts and crafts movement. The building was considered a *Gesamtkunstwerk*, or total work of art, because Behrens not only produced the architectural drawings but also designed the furniture, towels, paintings, pottery, and dishes.

Six years after his arts and crafts success, Behrens went to work as the artistic consultant for the German electronics company AEG. The company was a major manufacturer of generators, electric cables, light bulbs, and arc lamps. Although AEG was not considered a glamorous company, as Jeremy Aynsley wrote in *A Century of Graphic Design*, "this was among the most celebrated appointments in design history, as it heralded the birth of the corporate identity."[4]

At first, Behrens designed pamphlets, advertisements, and displays for international trade exhibitions. In 1908, however, he redesigned the corporate trademark to resemble a hexagonal honeycomb with the letters AEG printed in the designer's own elegant type font, Behrens-Antiqua. The logo was uniformly applied to all AEG printed graphics, buildings, and ads. It was also stamped on the company's new products, such as electric kettles, lamps, and fans. This was the first complete corporate identity scheme in graphic arts history, and as Aynsley wrote, it "led to a visual consistency in all AEG goods, which brought instant recognition by the consumer. Extensive use of Behrens-Antiqua gave the company's identity a clean, sober appearance and brought AEG praise for its systematic ordering of product information."[5]

Behrens was also a teacher, and his students spread his ideas on design throughout Europe and North America. Today the public image of nearly every corporation has its roots in Behrens's concept of integrated graphic design.

The Benefits of Good Design

Behrens was one of the first graphic designers to earn international recognition for his work. His success with AEG prompted ad agencies in the United States to recruit designers, fine artists, and illustrators who would create print ads and product packaging. These people were given job titles such as "consumer engineer" and "product stylist," and they were expected to generate demand for various products through the use of art and design.

Foremost among the consumer engineers was French-born illustrator Raymond Loewy, whose early work was inspired by the art deco movement. The term "art deco" originated in France in the mid-1920s and was characterized by illustrations of models with elongated torsos accompanied by geometric forms, sweeping curves, chevrons, and semicircular sunburst patterns meant to be elegant, stylish, and modern.

Loewy's career as an industrial designer began in 1929 when he was hired to change the look of the Gestetner copy machine. Loewy changed the look of the mundane machine by smoothing its shape and giving it the appearance of an object that moved swiftly such as an airplane or submarine, a design style called streamlining.

During the following four decades, Loewy streamlined hundreds of products, including toothbrushes, electric razors, the two-story Greyhound Scenic Cruiser bus, locomotives, and even the interiors of the Saturn and Skylab spacecrafts. In his efforts to streamline automobiles in the late 1940s, Loewy introduced now-standard design elements such as slanted windshields, built-in headlights, wheel covers, and lower, slimmer body designs. A classic example is the Loewy-designed 1953 Studebaker with a long nose. The car looked like it was moving quickly even when parked.

In the world of visual communications, Loewy redesigned the label and package for Lucky Strike cigarettes and streamlined the Coca-Cola bottle. He created logos for Exxon, Shell, Frigidaire, Nabisco, and the U.S. Postal Service. It is said that by 1951, a person could spend his or her entire day using products with graphics and designs styled by Raymond Loewy Associates. Commenting on the unending demand for his work, Loewy wrote, "Success finally came when we were able to convince some creative men that good appearance was a salable commodity, that it often cut costs, enhanced a product's prestige, raised corporate profits, benefited the customer and increased employment."[6]

Loewy died on July 14, 1986, at the age of 92. The occasion was marked by an outpouring of tributes concerning his contributions to graphic and industrial design. In the *New York Times*, reporter Susan Heller summed up the feeling of many in the design world: "One can hardly open a beer or a soft drink, fix breakfast, board a plane, buy gas, mail a letter or shop for an appliance without encountering a Loewy creation."[7]

Raymond Loewy streamlined the 1953 Studebaker so it gave the appearance of speed.

Design Is in Everything

Designers such as Loewy and Behrens became celebrities for their creative abilities, but countless anonymous graphic artists have influenced culture for generations. When looking at a dollar bill, an old National Geographic magazine, or an antique soda bottle, graphic arts act as living history by providing a window into the past. However, design is still very influential in the present day. Companies are constantly changing their websites, logos, and product designs in an effort to keep up with modern trends, and they need designers to help them figure out what will appeal to their customers.

CHAPTER TWO

Design in Books

Ever since books were invented, much care has gone into their design. In ancient times, manuscripts were written and illustrated by hand. After the invention of the printing press, different fonts were created in different parts of the world, based on the handwriting found in old manuscripts as well as the beliefs that were dominant in those regions. For instance, the first movable type was created in Germany in a style called Gothic. However, when the printing press was introduced in Italy, the Italians felt the Gothic style was too closely associated with religion. Many Italians in the Middle Ages followed the beliefs of Humanism—a school of thought that placed emphasis on secular, or nonreligious, philosophies. The Italian Humanists rejected the Gothic typeface and invented their own, which came to be called roman.

Over time, people changed the styles of fonts slightly, depending on what kind of idea they wanted their work to convey. When Apple created its first computers, Steve Jobs—one of the founders of the company—was inspired by a calligraphy class he took in college, so he asked designer Susan Kare to create several different fonts that would be available on the computer's word processing program. This is why computers come with different fonts. Today, there are thousands of different styles of fonts for designers to choose from, and the style of font can make a big difference in the way the viewer interprets the information they are seeing.

The first type of font ever created was called Gothic. The alphabet shown here is one example of a Gothic-style font.

Additionally, book designers today use programs such as Photoshop and InDesign to make sure the covers and interiors of books look pleasing to the reader's eye. Covers are especially important, since they are the first thing a potential reader sees. Although it is true that a reader cannot tell whether a book will be good or bad based on the cover, it is also true that someone is more likely to pick up a book with a cover that catches their eye. However, the interior is important as well because if a book is laid out poorly, the reader is less likely to keep reading it, no matter how good the content is. Designers must ensure that the cover snags a reader's interest and the interior keeps it.

Book Design Before Computers

Every day, thousands of books are published. They cover subjects such as art, cooking, entertainment, economics, business, computers, and history. Some books consist of words in black ink printed on cheap paper; others are large and expensive with beautiful color pictures on glossy paper. Whatever the style, the books require the work of graphic artists who lay out pages, position pictures, design attractive covers, and pick fonts. Much of this work is carried out on computers. However, long before the digital age, book artists performed these tasks with skilled hands and primitive tools.

The term "manuscript" is derived from the Latin *manu scriptus*, meaning "written by hand." In Europe, all books

Illuminated manuscripts were incredibly detailed and took months—sometimes years—to make.

were handwritten until the invention of the printing press in the mid-15th century. The earliest manuscripts were elaborately decorated religious works called codices (plural of codex), which consisted of folded sheets of paper secured between wooden boards. Most codices were created by Benedictine monks and were based on stories in the New Testament.

One of the oldest surviving codices is the Book of Kells. It features the four Gospels written in Latin. Irish monks who combined art, graphics, and medieval bookmaking technology created this elaborate and beautifully illustrated volume, called an illuminated manuscript, around AD 800. Like ancient Egyptian scrolls, the graphic design of the book is interlinear, which means images are placed between the lines of text. The text itself is embellished with decorated capital letters, borders, and small illustrations.

The Book of Kells is among thousands of illuminated manuscripts produced in Europe between the fifth and fifteenth centuries. While most were religious in nature, by the end of the Middle Ages, songbooks and books about biology, astronomy, and other sciences also appeared as illuminated manuscripts.

Illuminated manuscripts were often produced by monks who had the help of laypersons. Early graphic artists worked in a room dedicated to book production called a scriptorium, which means "the place for writing."

Because making a book by hand was a long, tedious process that could take a single individual at least six months, those working in scriptoria created manuscripts through a division of labor. With a team of workers possessing various skills, a copy could be created in about a month.

The first step in manuscript production involved cutting sheets of parchment to size. An apprentice drew lightly ruled lines on the paper. The basic layout was drawn in with silverpoint, a technique in which a graphic artist uses a pen with a tip of silver wire to draw a picture onto a piece of paper; which was then coated with gesso, a mixture of chalk and rabbit-skin glue. As the picture was drawn, the gesso picked up delicate lines of silver. Another artist, called a scribe, would carefully write out the words of the book in beautiful script known as calligraphy. The completed pages were turned over to a highly skilled illuminator, who painted images inside large letters at the beginning of each paragraph or page.

After illuminators decorated the letters, border painters created a variety of pictures and ornamentations. These paintings are called marginalia because they are in the margins of the pages. Commenting on the artistic quality of these pictures created in 15th–century Belgium, designer Norma Levarie wrote in *The Art and History of Books*, "The border-painters evolved a new type of border to go with the realistic miniature: a flat broad band, usually of gold, strewn with the most tangible blossoms and insects, painted with artful … shadows that make one feel that one could pick them up off the page."[8]

After the pages were completed, another designer would lay out the graphics for the leather cover, which might be decorated with floral designs, crests, or religious scenes. These would be impressed or engraved into the leather with metal or wood stamps. For those who could afford it, the cover designs could be made in gold tooling, a process in which a thin layer of gold was applied by hand. The cover and pages of the final product were turned over to bookbinders, who sewed the pages together on one side to create a strong binding.

Large scriptoria in northern Europe employed dozens of workers to create several manuscripts at a time. The works combined text, imagery, and ornamentation into masterpieces that were landmarks in visual communications. Reading was made easier by graphic design elements such as headings, punctuation, and capital letters.

Reproducing Books with Wooden Blocks

Illuminated manuscripts were artistic masterpieces that were expensive and rare; average Europeans rarely saw a book unless it was displayed in their church. However, around 1425, a technique imported from China and Japan called wood-block printing made books available to the masses for the first time.

Block printing involved sketching images and text, in reverse, onto blocks of beech wood. Expert woodcutters then carved the images into the blocks with chisels, knives, and files. The raised words and pictures were coated with ink and pressed onto paper.

Many wood-block books were filled with simple pictures and a few words to provide religious instruction and reading lessons to the illiterate, but others were masterpieces of graphic design. Illustrations were surrounded by columns and pillars that looked like the elaborate sculptures commonly carved onto church walls and public buildings. Short phrases of text appeared inside banners and ribbons to attract the eye.

The art of block books reached its pinnacle in 1493 with the publication of *The Nuremberg Chronicle*. This work, an illustrated history of Earth as told in the Bible—from creation to the 1490s—was illustrated and engraved by Michael Wolgemut, Wilhelm Pleydenwurff, and Albrecht Dürer. *The Nuremberg Chronicle*, printed in Nuremberg, Germany, contains 1,809 prints made from 645 woodcuts. The illustrations show religious scenes, villages, landscapes, everyday life, skeletons dancing, and people playing music.

Despite the intense labor required to carve dozens of sets of blocks, the book was so popular that between 1493

Expeditio in Bohemos hereticos facta temporibus Sigismundi

Martinus pontifex maxim⁹ vbi armatam heresim crescere indies animaduertit prius⁊ amplius inuale
sceret cardinalem vintoniensem natione anglicu regia stirpe natu in germania proficisci iussit.qui co
tra bohemicam labem in arma concurreret.Cui ⁊ imperator adiumento fuit. Instituti sunt tres exercitus
Saxonie duces.⁊ quos vocant stangnales ciuitates in primis militauere. Scdm ex franconibus constitu
tum marchio brandeburgensis duxauit.Tercio pfuit otto treuerensis archieps .que⁊ renenses secuti sunt
Baioarij quo⁊ ⁊ ciuitates sueuo⁊ imperiales ingressi bohemia tribus locis.silua penetrauere. iuncti sil
castrametati sunt.Sed cu heretici collecto raptim milite in eos pperare nunciaret no visum hoste fugerunt
No dum cardinalis exercitus affuerat fugientibus occurrens magnis pcibus vt redirent in hoste hortaf.
quod cu frustra niteret vir silua egressi superuenientes bohemi postremu agmen lacessere ceperut.facta e p/
fusior fuga.machinis quo⁊ bellicis potiti sunt.Exin misnia populati. Cu franconia redirent ne brandebur
gensem agru nurmbergensem⁊ vastarent pecunia placati diuite exercitu reduxere.Sigismundus his co
gnitis nurmberga pfectus noua principu auxilia coparat.Martinus quo⁊ pontifex maximus Iulianuz
cardinalem sancti angeli lris ac moribus excellentem cu ea legatione in teuthonia mittit vt bohemis bellu
inferat.⁊ aduentiente tpe in basiliensi pcilio quod pe die futuru erat noie aplico psideat. Is germania in
gressus mox nurmberga ad Sigismundu se confert.quo in loco frequentes germano⁊ principes conuene
rant.decreta est noua in bohemos expeditio ad octauu kal.iulij.Dux belli fridericus marchio brandebur
gensis declaratus.qui cardinalem sequeret . Ingressus bohemia in comitatu cardinalis.iohannes⁊ alber
tus principes brandeburgenses cu patre.Herbipolen.babenbergen.⁊ eysteten.epi.⁊ imperialiu ciuitatum
magistratus.Treuereii.⁊ colonien.antistites auxilia miserant.⁊ cu his puincia⁊ sua⁊ primores supra.xl.
milia equitu fuisse tradunf.Ingressus cardinalis numerosum exercitu ducens multas villas oppida⁊ he
retico⁊ diripuit.Bohemi qui iapridie hoste affuturu acceperant.expeditas in armis legiones coegerat.in
terea siue pditio in exercitu fidelium fuit(qd plurimi putauere)siue maius sua sponte metes boim pauor in
uasit totis castris trepidatu e.⁊ prius⁊ hostis vllus in pspectu daret sedissima capta fuga.mirat iulianus
vnde hic timor.Suaderet vt forti aio hoste expectaret.s frustra apud eos cohortatio fuit.sublata sunt ra
ptim signa ⁊ rapido cursu fuga maturauere.Hostis postea ex metu alieno ingenti pda potit⁹ e. Albert⁹ au
strie dux cu accepisset bohemia intrasse cardinale⁊raptim ex austria copijs in hereticos duxit.s fuga cogni
ta p morauia⁊ que no du eu pareb.at infesta signa circumferens.joo.villas ferro ⁊ igne deleuit.oppida vi cepit
mortaliu.maxima cede fecit.adeo⁊ gente illa afflixit vt iugu eius accipiens parere sibi ea lege promiserat
vt circa religione id sequi teneret qd basiliense concaliu decerneret.Exactus in bohemia legatus basileas se
contulit ibi⁊ concalium celebrauit.

Ordo nouus canonico⁊ regulariu ⁊ congregatio
sancte Iustine ⁊ Hieronimi

Ordo nouus canonico⁊ regulariu apud etruriaz
in lucesi agro monasterio frisonarie initiu sumpsit
a loco frisonaria dicta.deinde ab eugenio aucta laterane
sis appellata est.⁊ speciali priuilegio canonicis regula
ribus bti augustini aggregauit.Di a primo eo⁊ aucto
re clamide nigra cu nigro scapulari biretoq⁊ nigro sum
psere.⁊ albo scapulari xposito camisea linea eius loco
induere voluerunt.qua ob re vulgo fratres de la cami
sia pgnominauit.Habuerunt aut viros plurimos om
ni doctrina ⁊ eloquentia ⁊ sanctimonia celebres.

Congregatio etia sci benedicti que scte iustine nucu
pat hac tempestate in puincia taruisana apud pa
tauinu⁊be in monasterio scte iu stine primo p ludouicu
barbu patriciu veneti initiu seu reformatione accepit ⁊
ad via veritatis reduxit ⁊ ad regulare obseruantia pdu
xit.que congregatio viris pstantissimis ⁊ locis bonis⁊
ta tpalibus q⁊ spualibus excrescens.Eugenius quartus
pontifex ea maximis priuilegijs iuuit.deinde in ea innu
merabiles viri no modo iuriu ac sacre theologie doctri
na.sed et eloquentia litterarum tam grecaru q⁊ latinaru
ornatissimi fuerunt.

Ordo dni⁊ monachoru eremitar diui Hieronimi
⁊ a patru institutis collapsus a venerabili viro lu
po hispalensi eius ordinis generali pposito nouis insti
tutionibus ex dictis beati iheronimi instauratus e. qua
martino pape obtulit ⁊pontifex confirmauit.qui sub re
gula beati Benedicti militant.⁊ ipa p omnia viuit. nisi

The pictures in The Nuremberg Chronicle *were created with carved wooden blocks.*

and 1509 about 1,500 copies of *The Nuremberg Chronicle* were produced in Latin, while approximately 900 were printed in German. About 400 Latin and 300 German copies survive today.

Gutenberg's Printing Press

Wood-block manuscripts were the first step toward mass-produced books. However, even before *The Nuremberg Chronicle* was published, a milestone in graphic arts was achieved with the invention of movable metal type. Although many people worked on various aspects of this type of printing, credit for its invention is commonly given to Johannes Gutenberg, who built the first printing press in Mainz, Germany, around 1450. This machine allowed printers to produce several books a day.

According to the BBC documentary *The Medieval Mind: The Machine That Made Us*, "The printing press was the world's first mass-production machine. Its invention … changed the world as dramatically as splitting the atom or sending men into space, sparking a cultural revolution that shaped the modern age. It is the machine that made us who we are today."[9]

A Shortage of Books

Because creating a professional manuscript by hand was such a long and delicate process, relatively few books were made before the invention of the printing press, and the ones that were made were very expensive. In *The Art and History of Books*, Norma Levarie described how the scarcity of books affected life in 15th-century Europe:

> Copying manuscripts by hand was laborious and costly work. The books that existed were concentrated in the libraries of monasteries and universities, or in the rare private libraries that were the privilege of the very wealthy. A university such as Cambridge had only a hundred and twenty-two volumes in the year 1424. A private library at the end of the fifteenth century might boast of perhaps twenty volumes. A bound manuscript at that time cost as much money as an average court official received in a month. A scholar or student who was not exceptionally wealthy could only acquire books by copying them himself. The typical manuscript of the Middle Ages was not the splendid ornamented volume we know from reproductions or exhibitions; it was a hastily written copy made for practical use. In this time of scarcity … [people] needed books, and this need perhaps more than anything else brought about the beginning of printing.[1]

1. Norma Levarie, *The Art and History of Books*. Newcastle, DE: Oak Knoll, 1995, p. 67.

Although it was used for mass production, book printing was considered an art form. The first book to be produced with this new method was the famous Gutenberg Bible. Each page of the Bible contains 42 lines, and the entire book required more than 100,000 pieces of cast type. By the time the Bible was printed, Gutenberg was so far in debt that his press belonged to his business partners, who published the book.

The two-volume Gutenberg Bible sold for 300 florins, equal to three years' salary for an average clerk. However, this was considerably less than a handmade Bible, which could take a single monk 20 years to produce.

The next major project to come from Gutenberg's press was a Latin encyclopedia called the Mainz *Catholicon*. This work, written by religious scholar Johannes Balbus in the 13th century, was a long instruction manual detailing religious practices. A printer's note at the back proudly boasted of the method of its creation: "With the help of the Most High at whose will the tongues of infants become eloquent ... this noble book *Catholicon* has been printed and accomplished without the help of reed, stylus, or pen but by the wondrous agreement, proportion and harmony of [letter] punches and types."[10]

Without the invention of the printing press and movable type, books would still be rare and expensive items.

The creation of movable type was revolutionary. Each printing press required the skills of only 3 workers, and these printers could produce about 100 books a month. Within 10 years, typesetting technology had spread across Europe, and by 1500, there were thousands of printers in more than 200 cities in England, France, Italy, and the Netherlands. These printers engaged in a new field called job printing—producing pamphlets, calendars, religious writs, posters, and even playing cards. Some of this work was truly artistic, with printers using complicated four-color printing techniques invented by graphic designers who determined page layouts, typestyles, and ink colors.

Intaglio and Mezzotint

Like the Internet today, the printing press was a new technology that changed society. It came along during the Renaissance, when writers and artists were incorporating classical Greek philosophy and concepts of art into their work. In the field of graphics, designers turned their attention to the creation of different and distinctive sets of letters, numbers, and punctuation marks called typefaces, or fonts. During this era, the flowery Gothic typeface used by scribes—and reproduced by Gutenberg—was replaced with a simplified roman typeface similar to that used in ancient writing. In France, where King Francis I ordered all works to be printed in the roman type, a designer named Geoffroy Tory created an instruction manual to explain letter shapes, spelling rules, and the use of accents, quotation marks, and the apostrophe.

The title of Tory's book, *Champ Fleury*, is a French term that translates as the "flowery fields." This expressive title was a result of the author's philosophy that stated the shapes of letters should be based on the proportions of the human body. This is explained in the book's subtitle: *The Art and Science of the Proportion of the Attic or Ancient Roman Letters, According to the Human Body and Face*.

Tory was a scholar, editor, scribe, illuminator, and bookseller. To lay out perfectly proportioned letters, he designed a square grid that foreshadowed the method used for type design in the 20th century. It is also the basis for the pixels of computerized letterforms. Tory's detailed letters had to be reproduced with refined printing methods, so his books were published with a process called intaglio, which is Italian for "to carve." Intaglio allows graphic artists to cut, or engrave, illustrations into copper plates that are used for printing.

Although it is an ancient technique, intaglio did not come into use in Europe until the 15th century. Another intaglio process, mezzotint, or "half tint," allowed artists to create a rich range of gray tones between black and white and was ideal for printing portraits. To create a mezzotint, the artist uses a metal

Words and illustrations created with the mezzotint process appear as a series of tiny dots.

tool with small teeth that roughs up the plate with thousands of tiny dots that hold ink.

The intaglio process opened up yet another avenue for graphic artists, allowing just about any illustration to be printed. This set the stage for a wave of publishing that included scientific and medical illustrations as well as books of art and music. However, the process could not be used on the same page as type, so books had illustrations on one page with the text on the opposite page.

The intaglio process reached its high point with the publication of Denis Diderot's *Encyclopédie* between 1751 and 1772. The 17 volumes of printed text were accompanied by 11 volumes of illustrations, or plates. Diderot believed "a glance at an object or its representation is more informative than a page of text."[11]

Medieval Versus Modern Printing

Johannes Gutenberg was a jeweler who understood processes involving carving and metal casting. When he invented the printing press, the major innovation was the method he created for molding letters, or type. Gutenberg made what is called a "punch" from steel that contained the mirror image of a letter. The punch was hammered into copper, a softer metal, to make a mold that was filled with a melted mixture of lead, tin, and antimony. This alloy, or metal mixture, was specially formulated by Gutenberg to melt easily and harden quickly. The resulting cast pieces of type could be put together to form words, sentences, and paragraphs when fit into a rack. To print the page, the type in the rack was coated with a special ink made from linseed oil and soot, developed to stick to the metal. Paper was laid on the inked type, and the rack was rolled into the printing press. The screw was turned to lower a plate in a firm, even pressure so the images of the letters were transferred onto the paper.

Today, two main types of printing are used. Offset printing is similar to Gutenberg's original design; an offset printer is automated, but still "uses etched metal plates that apply ink onto a sheet of paper."[1] This type of printing is expensive unless more than 2,000 items are being printed. For smaller batches, digital printing is more cost-effective because it requires less time and material. A digital printer "uses electrostatic rollers—called 'drums'—to apply toner onto the paper ... The toner is then ... fused—passed through a high-heat unit—onto the paper."[2]

1. Andrew Shu, "What's the Difference Between Offset Printing versus Digital Printing?," MGX Copy, May 27, 2014. www.mgxcopy.com/blog/san-diego-printing/2014/05/27/whats-difference-offset-printing-versus-digital-printing/.
2. Shu, "What's the Difference Between Offset Printing versus Digital Printing?"

The Automation of the Printing Industry

The number of new fonts coincided with a growing demand for books throughout the 19th century. Nearly every aspect of book production in Europe and the United States was changing rapidly due to the Industrial Revolution. It was an era of factories, automation, and mass production driven by the invention of the steam engine. Around 1820, Gutenberg's old-style, hand-operated wooden press was replaced by steam-powered presses that allowed press operators to produce more than 1,000 pages per hour. In the 1830s, the invention of automatic type casters allowed a worker to make up to 20,000 pieces of type a day.

In the 1880s, several inventions that appeared within a few years of each other once again revolutionized the book arts. In the 1880s, German inventor Ottmar Mergenthaler invented the linotype machine. Since Gutenberg's day, printers had been using hundreds of individual letters to form sentences and paragraphs. The linotype, which could be operated by one person, fused the letters into a long, solid line, or slug, of molten lead. The slugs could later be melted down and the lead reused to make more type.

In the 1850s, the halftone printing process was invented, and advancements were made to it throughout the next century and a half. Halftone printing allowed printers to reproduce photographs as a series of black-and-white dots with full ranges of gray. Before this method was developed, photographic prints had to be pasted onto individual pages of books, an awkward and expensive process. With the introduction of halftones, books with photographs of exotic locations, war zones, and scientific subjects were instant best sellers, and publishers could barely keep up with public demand.

The New Typography: Simplifying Style

New technology changed the look of books. However, as printers focused on mass production, the quality of graphic design suffered; pages became hard to read due to long, dense lines of type and small margins. This began to change in the 1920s with the advent of the new typography movement in Germany. Calligrapher and printer Jan Tschichold, one of the leading voices of new typography, wanted to formalize rules of book design that emphasized clarity, arrangement, and readability.

Tschichold believed that typographers should abandon the decorative serif fonts of the so-called old typography movement and adopt type without serifs, or sans serif. In October 1925, he summarized his views in the manifesto "Elementary Typography" in the German trade magazine *Typographic News*:

> *The new typography emphasizes function. The goal of every typography is communication …*

Communication must appear in the shortest, simplest and most forceful form ... The basic typeface form is the sans serif typeface in all variations: light, semibold, bold, condensed to extended. Typefaces that ... are not elementally designed ... limit the possibility of international understanding.[12]

These words may not sound very exciting today, but they created controversy in the graphic arts community while making Tschichold famous. Many typesetters were at first reluctant to abandon the old typestyles, but within a few years, ornamental fonts disappeared from books. Serifs, however, did not disappear completely; they simply became smaller, making the letters easier to read. For instance, this book is printed in a serif font. Many people believe serif fonts are easier to read than sans serif ones, but no scientific studies have proven this conclusively.

Tschichold also believed that books were difficult to read when each line was centered on the page. While this symmetry had long been viewed by old typographers as beautiful and harmonious, Tschichold advocated for asymmetry. He thought that sentences should be flush left, that is, aligned on the left but of various lengths on the right. This design was meant to attract and hold the viewer's attention. According to the website UX Movement, which features articles about the ways design choices affect a website user's experience,

"Left aligned text is easier to read than centered text for paragraphs. This is because when you center your text, the starting place of each line changes. This forces your users to work harder to find where each line begins to continue reading."[13] Today, nearly every publication aligns its text to the left for this reason.

A Return to Tradition

Tschichold's ideas may seem unexciting, but in 1932, they were a radical change from tradition. When the Nazis came to power in Germany, they were threatened by any kind of change; instead, they wanted to strengthen old traditions. For this reason, they accused Tschichold of "being a 'cultural Bolshevik [Communist]' and creating 'un-German' typography."[14] They seized his works, saying they were threatening the well-being of the German people. The calligrapher fled to England, where he went to work in 1947 as a designer for Penguin Books. He developed the Penguin Composition Rules to standardize the look of the books. The rules covered text composition, indenting paragraphs, punctuation, the use of capitals and italics, and rules for footnotes and references.

The founder of Penguin, Allen Lane, wanted to make quality literature available to the public for the same price as a pack of cigarettes. To reach the widest market, Penguin sold its books out of vending machines in general stores and subway stations rather than bookstores. This concept revolutionized graphic

A Note from the Designer

Seth Hughes, the designer who worked on this book, described the graphic design process and how he approaches projects such as this one:

Being a graphic designer means having the ability to examine a complex idea or situation and then break it down into its purest, most essential parts. How do you tell a story or express an idea or emotion with a few short strokes of a pen? Take a logo design, for instance. Designers have to first gather as much information as they can on their client to produce a successful logo. They need to ask "Who's the client?," "What do they make?," and "Who wants to buy what they sell and why?" Once the designer has all this information, they're better suited to decide what's valuable and, more importantly, what is of little worth. No designer works exactly like another, but typically deciding what's important and what isn't involves some form of brainstorming and sketching possible solutions. Usually a good designer will be able to articulate a few rough solutions using these creative methods.

Finishing a design requires an understanding of the principles and elements of design. Shape, repetition, texture, hierarchy, balance and color are just a few examples. It can be difficult to understand exactly why people find certain visual cues aesthetically pleasing, but the principles and elements help the designer compose and polish their finished product. The book you're reading, as an example, capitalizes on many of the principles and elements of design. Rough paint splash-like shapes and textures are repeated throughout the book to impart a sense of craft and playfulness. The same few colors are echoed on nearly every page. A limited color scheme helps to navigate the reader's eye from page to page without being prominent enough to overpower the content. The sizes and colors of titles, subtitles and body fonts are carefully chosen to establish a hierarchy of visual importance. These pieces are composed to bring balance and purpose to the book, visually.

Lastly, a design isn't done until the client approves. It can be a little discouraging to hear criticism about a piece, but a good designer will take it in stride and use it as an opportunity to better themselves and their craft.[1]

1. Seth Hughes, e-mail interview by author, February 28, 2017.

arts once again because the book covers featured bright colors coded for book content, which was meant to attract maximum interest among products sold in stores. Lane took this idea, as well as the idea of naming the company after a bird, from a German publishing company called Albatross Verlag. All of Penguin's books featured two bands of color with a white stripe in the middle. Orange meant the book was general fiction, green was crime fiction, pink was travel and adventure, blue was biography, red was drama, purple was essays, and yellow was for things that did not fit a specific category.

The genres of Penguin books were easily recognizable by the color of the covers.

Tschichold remained a guiding force in book design. In Germany, his ideas about the new typography created a design revolution; in England, he led a revival of tradition that soon spread to other countries. He still believed that sans serif fonts and left-aligned text were the best way to create advertisements as well as information relating to art and architecture, but he felt long pages of sans serif were too hard to read and did not give the right tone to poetry and literature. For this reason, "he believed designers should draw upon the whole history of design to create solutions expressing content. While much of his later work used symmetrical organization and classical serif type styles he advocated freedom of thought and artistic expression."[15]

While advances in technology changed the methods used to produce books over the years, Tschichold's rules remain popular. They are widely used today by graphic artists designing books, magazines, newspapers, and websites.

A Design Renaissance

Penguin's cover designs were popular because they were easy to understand. However, other publishers were not able to use the same idea, so they had to think of different ways to design their covers that would make people want to read their books. Throughout most of the 20th century, publishers used illustrations that showed exactly what the book was about. These often featured the main characters standing in a setting or performing an action that was important to the plot of the book. In the 1960s and 1970s, some publishers experimented with abstract or minimalist designs, including covers that contained no pictures, only the title of the book. On these covers, font, color, shape, and hierarchy—the way the designer arranged the letters to draw the viewer's eye in a certain direction—were important factors in creating a unique, striking design. However, many books still had the illustrated covers.

Near the end of the 20th century, cover design took an interesting turn. Designers such as Chip Kidd and Rodrigo Corral began combining different design elements to create covers that were bold and eye-catching. Some of these covers gave a symbolic idea of what the book was about; for instance, Kidd's famous cover for *Jurassic Park* shows a *Tyrannosaurus rex* skeleton. Others are simply designed to stand out from the other covers on a shelf. For example, Corral's cover for a book called *Paris, I Love You but You're Bringing Me Down* is very simple, with a solid red cover, white capital letters, and two symbols (the word "love" is replaced with a heart and the word "down" is replaced with an arrow pointing down). According to graphic designer Robert Bieselin, cover art is more important in the age of e-readers than it was in the past because "on-location book sales are lower, competition is steeper, and shelf space [is] smaller, all of which has forced publishers to reinvent [book cover design]."[16]

Nearly everyone has seen Chip Kidd's book cover designs in stores and libraries. The dinosaur graphic he created for the Jurassic Park book cover was also used for the movie poster (seen below).

Since many people order books online, designers face the challenge of making covers that look good even as small pictures, called thumbnails, on a website.

Book design has advanced technologically since the days of the monks writing in their scriptoria, and some of its goals have changed as well. In the Middle Ages, when books were scarce and expensive, designers focused on making a book as beautiful as they could. After the invention of the printing press, when books became more widely available and readers had many choices, designers had to think of creative ways to make readers choose their book over all the others. Today, book covers are a form of advertisement, but often they are also miniature works of art.

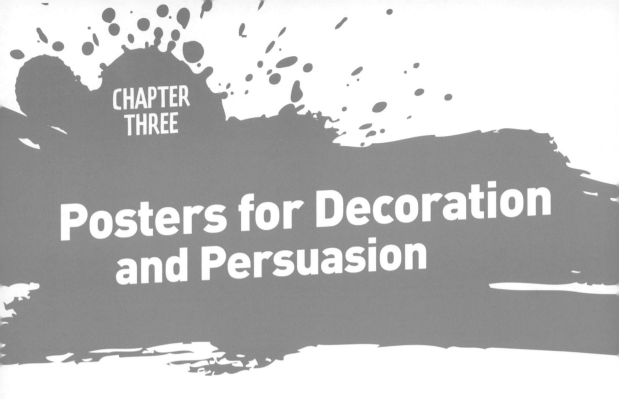

Posters for Decoration and Persuasion

Posters are everywhere in today's society. They are used to sell items; advertise concerts, plays, and other forms of entertainment; and convince people to think a certain way about something. Posters can be seen in homes, on the walls of public buildings, on telephone poles, and many other places. Graphic designers must work hard to catch someone's eye so their poster does not blend in with all the others.

Posters first began to be used in France in the second half of the 19th century. They were meant to be used as advertisements, but the artists who created them were so talented that they were soon sought after by art collectors. Poster artists experimented with new styles, which influenced artists in the generations to come.

Experimentation with Grease, Water, and Ink

Like many advances in the graphic arts, the rise of the poster can be traced to the invention of a new technology. In this case it was lithography, Greek for "stone printing," which was discovered in 1798 by Alois Senefelder, an Austrian playwright. Senefelder was driven to his discovery by sheer necessity. Although he had written one successful play, he found he was too poor to pay a printer to publish his second play. In an effort to print the play himself, Senefelder experimented unsuccessfully with various methods, using etched stones and metal plates. One day as he was puzzling over his conundrum, his mother called out a long list of items she wanted him to pick up when he went out. Lacking a sheet of

Lithographic prints are created using a roller to transfer an image from stone to paper.

paper, Senefelder picked up a grease pencil and scribbled his mother's list on a flat printing stone he had nearby.

The writing element of Senefelder's grease pencil was made from oil-based wax and black pigment. After he used it on the stone, he realized a basic scientific principle: Oil and water do not mix. Eventually, he devised the lithographic method. He drew an image on a stone with the grease pencil and then spread water over the entire stone. This moistened all the areas except the grease image, which repelled the water. An oil-based ink was rolled over the stone, but it only stuck to the image. A sheet of paper was placed over the illustration, a roller was applied, and the image was transferred to the paper.

Senefelder's lithography was the first new printing technology since Gutenberg's press. He soon realized that by using three stones with three colors—blue, red, and yellow—he could print an infinite variety of blended colors. Commenting on the possibilities of three-color lithography in his 1819 book *The Invention of Lithography*, Senefelder wrote:

If this [process] is done just right, and if, of course, the drawing bears the impress of a masterly hand, and if the printer understands his art, the impression will be perfectly like an original drawing, so that the most skilled etcher in copper hardly can attain the same effect. Therefore this method, which has the further advantage of being a quick one, is excellently well adapted for copying paintings.[17]

A Lucky Accident

In the 1890s, artist and illustrator Alphonse Mucha was one of the most famous graphic designers in the world, and the French referred to an entire artistic style as *le Style Mucha*. He found fame accidentally:

On Christmas Eve 1894, Mucha was at the Lemerciers' printing company, dutifully correcting proofs for a friend who had taken a holiday. Suddenly the printing firm's manager burst into the room, upset because the famous actress Sarah Bernhardt was demanding a new poster for the play Gismonda *by New Year's Day. As Mucha was the only artist available, he received the commission ... [Mucha] used Byzantine-inspired mosaics as background motifs, and produced a poster totally distinct from any of his prior work. The bottom portion of this poster was unfinished because only a week was available for design, printing, and posting.*[1]

Parisians immediately fell in love with Mucha's work, and he became famous almost overnight. His work helped shape what came to be called the art nouveau movement, which had a huge impact on poster design.

1. Philip B. Meggs and Alston W. Purvis, *Meggs' History of Graphic Design.* Hoboken, NJ: John Wiley & Sons, Inc., 2012, p. 211.

Mucha's Gismonda *poster made him famous almost instantly, even though he had so little time to do it that the bottom portion remained unfinished.*

Jules Chéret and
les Chérettes

Lithography allowed artists and illustrators, for the first time, to draw their designs directly onto the printing surface. This meant those unfamiliar with intaglio could reproduce detailed designs quickly and easily. By the 1840s, further advances in the lithographic process allowed designers to print amazingly realistic imagery. This method was used to publish graphics of every description, including maps, portraits, historical scenes, product labels, and even Christmas cards. Elaborate designs could use up to 40 different stones to achieve intricate, layered imagery.

The most competitive field in lithography was the printing of advertisement posters called signboards. These could be produced at the rate of 10,000 sheets per hour. Lithographers could make large posters about 32 by 46 inches (81 by 117 cm), whereas the average printing press could only produce work 10 by 15 inches (25 by 38 cm) in size.

In this era before movies and television, people found entertainment at carnivals, circuses, expositions, concerts, and plays. There was fierce competition for the public's money, and posters were the bait that promoters used to attract customers. In this competitive environment, printing firms hired the leading artists and illustrators of the day to create attractive, eye-catching posters. One Parisian painter and lithographer, Jules Chéret, did not see posters simply as an opportunity to sell something, but also as a way for an artist to exercise his or her creativity. His work established lithography as the leading creative medium of the day, so he is now known as the father of the modern poster.

Chéret's career began in 1849 when he was 13 and his father bought him a 3-year apprenticeship in a Paris lithography shop. After studying art and lithography in France and Britain, he established a Paris lithography firm in 1866. When he printed a large theatrical poster for a production featuring world-famous actress Sarah Bernhardt, it was the first visual poster of its type.

In 1881, Chéret sold his firm but remained the company's art director. This allowed him to spend his days designing and drawing his illustrations on lithographic stones. He perfected a technique to print his work in sections, which allowed his printers to produce posters that were 7 feet (2 m) high. The press run on a single poster might have been as many as 200,000 copies in a year.

Chéret's graphic designs featured a bright range of attention-grabbing colors with details filled in with stipples (dot patterns) and crosshatching (short intersecting lines). Rather than using lines of standard type, he often drew his letters freehand, arching the words around central figures or splashing letters across the page.

Chéret's design innovations were responsible for major changes in

The girls Chéret drew, called les Chérettes, *became role models for Parisian women in the early 1900s.*

French culture and fashion in an era known as *la belle époque,* or the beautiful era, a term used to describe the fabulous nightlife of Paris. Chéret's posters featured dancers kicking up their heels, peering over their shoulders, spinning, and flying through the air. The high-stepping models looked happy and excited, symbols of the carefree Paris nightlife. When the posters appeared by the thousands on the walls of Paris, young women imitated the looks of the Chéret girls, or *les Chérettes.* At this point in history, women were expected to be proper and ladylike at all times; anyone who did not conform to society's standards was considered to have loose morals. The *Chérettes* were women who wore low-cut dresses, danced, drank alcohol, and smoked in public, but it was clear that they were doing these things because they enjoyed them, not to attract men's attention. They became role models of feminism for Parisian women.

Because of his work, Chéret was awarded the highest decoration a Frenchman can receive: He was named to the Legion of Honor for "creating a new branch of art that advanced printing and served the needs of commerce and industry."[18] There was only one problem with the public's love of his work: The posters were often stolen off the walls as quickly as they were put up. However, due to massive print runs, some of the originals are still available for purchase today.

Art Nouveau

Chéret's main competition in the 1890s was French painter and illustrator Henri de Toulouse-Lautrec. Lautrec mainly drew dancers in Paris cabarets, or nightclubs. However, unlike Chéret's dancing women, Lautrec's seemed sad and lonely. His fans were impressed with his ability to show that kind of emotion in his drawings.

Unlike Chéret, who produced more than 1,000 designs, Lautrec's poster production was limited to only 31. This succeeded in making his limited illustrations more attractive to art collectors and helped spark what was called "poster mania" in the 1890s.

However, Lautrec's influence went beyond the commercial market of art buyers and sellers. His use of radically flat figures, silhouettes, symbolic shapes, and expressive imagery inspired a generation of poster artists, and the streets of Paris served as their art gallery.

The poster fad coincided with the art nouveau ("new art") movement that was also gripping France. This highly decorative style was characterized by flowing, curved lines and ornamental flower or plant patterns. It was called "new art" because it did not take inspiration from past design; instead, artists looked at what was around them, especially in nature. Educator and designer Philip B. Meggs provided a description of the style:

Art Nouveau's identifying visual quality is an organic, plantlike

Art nouveau was characterized by flowing lines as well as patterns of vines and flowers. Many of the entrances to the Paris metro (subway) stations remain in the art nouveau style.

line. *Freed from roots and gravity, [the line] can either undulate with whiplash energy or flow with elegant grace as it defines, modulates, and decorates a given space. Vine tendrils, flowers (such as the rose and lily), birds (particularly peacocks), and the human female form were frequent motifs [reoccurring themes] from which this fluid line was adapted.*[19]

Art nouveau, a style based on the British arts and crafts movement, was popular in France between 1890 and 1910. Proponents of the movement attempted to remove the dividing line between art and audience, believing that everything should be art. To make their point, they put the art nouveau style on wallpaper, Paris metro stations, dishes, clothing, light fixtures, doorways, and stained glass.

"Keep Calm and Carry On"

When World War II broke out, England prepared several propaganda posters to boost the morale of its citizens. Two of these were posted all across Britain, urging citizens to defend freedom and to stay brave and cheerful. Both posters featured capital letters on a solid-colored background with the image of a crown above them. The third poster, which said "Keep Calm and Carry On," was never posted during the war, but it ended up becoming the most popular and well-known of the set. According to *Business Insider*,

Around 2.5 million copies were printed, but not one of them was posted, as officials had last-minute doubts about whether the content was too patronizing or obvious. They also couldn't settle on an appropriate time to hang the posters. Save for a select few, the majority of the posters were destroyed.

Fast-forward six decades [to the year 2000] and one of the remaining posters was discovered by a bookseller who bought a box of old books (where the poster was hidden) at auction. It was put up over the cash register in the seller's bookshop, Northumberland's Barter Books.[1]

Customers loved the poster and asked where they could get copies, so the owners began printing them. Today, the poster has been copied and parodied millions of times, sometimes to the point where it barely resembles the original.

1. Brittany Fowler, "Brits May Roll Their Eyes at 'Keep Calm and Carry On'—but Here's Why They Secretly Love It," *Business Insider*, June 23, 2015. www.businessinsider.com/the-surprising-history-of-keep-calm-and-carry-on-2015-6.

Propaganda Posters

Art nouveau crossed the ocean to the United States around 1900 and was prominently featured on the covers of *Harper's* and other magazines. However, poster mania had run its course in France, and many of the famous poster artists moved on to other projects.

By the 1910s, *la belle époque* also faded into history, replaced by a modern era of electric lights, airplanes, automobiles, and heavy machinery. In many cases, the lithographic process was replaced by the updated printing press, which could reproduce posters faster, more cheaply, and in greater quantity.

The growing industrialization of Europe also allowed nations to build new, deadly machines of war. This led to tragic results in 1914 when World War I broke out, with Germany and Austria-Hungary on one side and France and Great Britain on the other.

During the war, which eventually involved the United States and Canada as well as numerous European nations, governments had to achieve several goals. They needed to recruit soldiers, raise money to finance the war, and convince people to conserve, plant vegetable gardens, and recycle to prevent shortages of important resources. In addition, governments created propaganda to turn people against the enemy by making their actions seem evil and declaring that they threatened civilization. In this era before radio or television, the task of communicating these objectives to the public fell to poster artists.

At the outbreak of the war, Germany was a world leader in printing technology and graphic design, so it is not surprising that they were the first to produce propaganda posters. Their style was based on the *sachplakat*, or object poster, invented in Germany in 1906 by graphic designer Lucian Bernhard. The object poster reduces design elements to a minimum, featuring a product in flat colors, a logo with solid shadows, and a line or two of bold type, usually in hand-drawn block letters.

Bernhard originally designed the *sachplakat* to stand out among the art nouveau posters that were plastered on nearly every wall and fence in Berlin. However, when he used these design techniques on a poster for a 1915 war loan campaign, the results must surely have frightened Germany's enemies. Reprinted in international graphics magazines, the poster features the clenched fist of a medieval knight, wearing armored gloves that resemble brass knuckles. The lettering, in a Gothic typeface, says, "This [meaning the fist] is the way to peace—the enemy wills it so! Thus subscribe to the war loan!"[20]

Messages of Patriotism

The Americans and British took a different approach to wartime posters, relying on vivid painted illustrations rather than stark graphics. However, the goal was the same—to inspire fear and hatred of the enemy. A poster designed by respected illustrator

Joseph Pennell for the Fourth Liberty Loan bond drive in 1918 was typical of the era. It shows the Statue of Liberty surrounded by bright orange flames and New York City in the background, also in flames. Overhead, German airplanes fly through the sky dropping bombs. Beneath this menacing picture, black capital letters in a gold box state,

"THAT LIBERTY SHALL NOT PERISH FROM THE EARTH

BUY LIBERTY BONDS."

Pennell's poster was one of the most popular of the war, and the illustrator emphasized the importance of graphic arts during wartime: "When the United States wished to make public its wants, whether of men or money, it found that art—as the European countries had found—was the best medium."[21]

By far the most recognizable image from the era is the military recruitment poster *I Want You for U.S. Army*, showing Uncle Sam—who got his name from the United States's initials—with his white goatee and top hat, pointing a long index finger at the viewer. Five million copies were printed of this poster designed by graphic artist James Montgomery Flagg, and it is one of the most recognizable graphic images of the 20th century. It was among the first of many posters directly addressing the viewer.

Like many well-known works of art, James Montgomery Flagg's illustration has been parodied countless times over the years. During the Vietnam War era, a group of antiwar graphic designers formed the Committee to Help Unsell the War. Their 1971 contribution showed a bruised and bloodied Uncle Sam reaching out his hand with the caption, "I Want Out."

The Uncle Sam poster is so famous that it has been parodied countless times, including in antiwar posters and even in posters depicting characters created by writer H.P. Lovecraft.

I WANT YOU FOR CTHULHU WORSHIP

NEAREST BOOK OF LOVECRAFT

In more recent times, artist Stephen Kroninger protested the Gulf War of 1991 by showing President George H.W. Bush as Uncle Sam. The typography in the poster consisted of cut out letters resembling a kidnapper's ransom note. The caption read, "Uncle George Wants You to Forget Failing Banks, Education, Drugs, AIDS, Poor Health Care, Unemployment, Crime, Racism, Corruption, and Have a Good War."

Eleven years later, the website TomPaine.com ran a parody meant to protest the Iraq War. Uncle Sam was replaced on the recruiting poster with terrorist mastermind Osama bin Laden, or "Uncle oSAMa." Indicating that the war in Iraq would help recruit more terrorists, Osama bin Laden pointed his finger and said, "I Want You to Invade Iraq."

Not all the parodies of this poster are political; some use images from pop culture, including a picture of Darth Vader saying, "I Want You for the Imperial Guard" and a picture of Batman's nemesis, the Joker, saying, "I Want You to Laugh." Whatever the cause, the Uncle Sam graphic design proves that a classic image can be timeless and used to communicate many different ideas over the years.

Rosie the Riveter

In the mid-1930s, as the threat of World War II was growing, the poster was once again drafted into the service of conquest. In Germany, the Nazis were masters of propaganda, and their leader, Adolf Hitler, consciously created fear-provoking symbols to represent his regime graphically. These included the right-facing German imperial eagle and the black swastika on a field of red and white. However, after the war began in 1939, German cities were under aerial bombardment, which disrupted the ability of the Nazis to produce propaganda.

In the United States, the power of the poster was well understood during World War II. By this time, technology had advanced to the point where posters could be mass-produced through offset printing rather than lithography. This change in printing style limited the number of colors that could be used, which resulted in an effect known as posterization: The gradients (shading) of the image change abruptly rather than gradually, so there is less detail in the image.

In the early days of fighting, the government set up a special unit, the Office of Wartime Information, to employ graphic designers, illustrators, and artists for the cause. These people created posters that were placed in libraries, post offices, schools, factories, and other public places. The World War II Poster Collection from the Northwestern University Library website explained the many important themes featured in posters of World War II:

Some address home efforts for conservation of materials and rationing; others exhort workers to

Are you a girl with a Star-Spangled heart?

The United States used posters such as this one and the one on the next page to encourage women to work or volunteer during World War II.

JOIN THE **WAC** NOW!

THOUSANDS OF ARMY JOBS NEED FILLING!

Women's Army Corps
United States Army

The more WOMEN at work the sooner we WIN!

WOMEN ARE NEEDED ALSO AS:

FARM WORKERS	WAITRESSES	TIMEKEEPERS	LAUNDRESSES
TYPISTS	BUS DRIVERS	ELEVATOR OPERATORS	TEACHERS
SALESPEOPLE	TAXI DRIVERS	MESSENGERS	CONDUCTORS

— and in hundreds of other war jobs!

SEE YOUR LOCAL U.S. EMPLOYMENT SERVICE

58 *Graphic Design: Putting Art and Words Together*

OWI Poster No. 59.   Additional copies may be obtained upon request from the Division of Public Inquiries, Office of War Information, Washington, D.C.   ☆ U.S. GOVERNMENT PRINTING OFFICE : 1943—O-517134

greater productivity and quality output; while others warn of the dangers of innocently leaking critical defense information to unsuspected enemy agents. Women are encouraged to work in factories or military support positions, and instructed how to behave in these situations. Some of the posters are targeted directly at school children, including charts illustrating how specific savings amounts could outfit the equipment and supplies needed by a brave G.I. soldier. Various [poster] series address themes such as nutrition or investment in war bonds.[22]

The posters that urged women to work had patriotic themes, showing secretaries behind their typewriters saluting the viewer. Others played on the emotional aspect of the conflict, such as Lawrence Wilbur's illustration of a distressed woman above the caption "Longing Won't Bring Him Back Sooner … Get a War Job!" However, one of the most enduring images from this era highlighted the strengths of women. J. Howard Miller's *We Can Do It!* features Rosie the Riveter, a woman dressed in overalls and bandanna, flexing the muscles of her right arm. As the National Archives explained, the image in the poster was meant to change longstanding societal ideas about women: "[Rosie] was introduced as a symbol of patriotic womanhood. The accoutrements of war work—uniforms, tools, and lunch pails—were

incorporated [to revise the] image of the feminine ideal."[23]

Although many posters of this era focused on what Americans could do to help the war effort, some showed the enemy in an unfavorable light. Posters focusing on the Japanese were particularly racist, often showing a character called the "Tokio Kid," a Japanese man with claws, fangs, and exaggeratedly small eyes. The captions were written in grammatically incorrect English, and the typeface was meant to look similar to Japanese writing called kanji. These posters were intended to make Americans see the Japanese as less than human so they would feel better about going to war with them.

However, this campaign worked so well that it had an unfortunate consequence: The posters increased the suspicions Americans had toward anyone who looked Japanese. In 1942, the federal government ordered about 110,000 Japanese-Americans to be forced into relocation camps, where they stayed for almost 4 years. People believed during World War II that anyone who looked Japanese was a potential threat. Many of the people who were sent to the camps had never even seen Japan, and all of them were loyal American citizens. The propaganda posters did not create racism against the Japanese, but they exacerbated, or made worse, the anti-Japanese feelings that led to the internment order. This shows that good design is not always used for a good purpose.

A Symbol of Peace

I n the mid-1960s, graphic art exploded off the printed page, where it had been for 1,000 years, and onto buttons, bumper stickers, and T-shirts. One of the most widespread examples of this graphic arts revolution was the peace sign.

The symbol representing peace was actually a product of the 1950s. It was designed by British graphic arts professional Gerald Holtom for a 1958 London peace march that was organized by the Direct Action Committee Against Nuclear War, which later helped form a group called Campaign for Nuclear Disarmament. Holtom had convinced the groups that their message would have a greater impact if they had a simple visual image. The designer used two letters from the semaphore, or military flag-signaling, alphabet. He overlaid the symbol for the letter N (nuclear) over the letter D (disarmament). Holtom placed the letters in a circle that represented Earth.

The peace symbol was imported into the United States by Philip Altbach, a member of the Student Peace Union (SPU), a college antiwar group formed in the late 1950s. The SPU sold thousands of peace symbol buttons on college campuses. By 1967, when the anti-Vietnam War movement was growing rapidly, the peace symbol seemed to be everywhere. The graphic symbol of peace remains popular today, especially among protesters.

The Psychedelic Era

In the mid-1960s, thousands of young adults in San Francisco began experimenting with lysergic acid diethylamide (LSD, or acid) and other psychedelic drugs after attending parties called "acid tests." These events were organized by the Merry Pranksters, a group of rebels led by Ken Kesey, the best-selling author of *One Flew Over the Cuckoo's Nest*. LSD was legal at the time, and the events were publicized with posters unlike any ever seen before. Norman Hartweg's *Can You Pass the Acid Test?* poster advertised the parties and entertainment such as the band the Grateful Dead and the poet Allen Ginsburg. Every space on the poster is filled with random images such as comic book figures, as well as silly, nonsensical comments. The freeform, flowing lettering on the poster is shaded with stripes, checks, spots, paisley patterns, and American flags. While this hand-drawn poster is raw and amateurish, it set the stage for the poster revolution that was to follow.

The acid tests ended in October 1966 when LSD was outlawed in California. However, a handful of largely unschooled artists who had attended the acid tests remade the world of visual design. Alton Kelly, Stanley Mouse, Victor Moscoso, Robert "Wes" Wilson, and Rick Griffin began designing posters for rock concerts and covers for record albums. They used swirling lines, Victorian imagery, Native American designs, and art nouveau fonts.

Wilson said he used colors and patterns taken from his visual experiences with LSD. Moscoso used sharply contrasting lines that created optical illusions such as afterimages on the retina and other distortions meant to imply a drug experience. Mouse and Kelly, who worked together, spent hours in the San Francisco library paging through old books from the 1800s, taking imagery from Native American photographs. One of their most famous images, a skull with a crown of red roses made for the Grateful Dead, first appeared on the band's second album in 1971. Before his death in 2008, Kelly told the *San Francisco Chronicle*,

Stanley and I had no idea what we were doing. But we went ahead and looked at American Indian stuff, Chinese stuff, Art Nouveau, Art Deco, Modern … whatever. We were stunned by what we found and what we were able to do. We had free rein to just go graphically crazy. Where before that, all advertising was pretty much just typeset with a photograph of something.[24]

Rather than use set type around this combination of wild imagery, the poster artists went out of their way to make the words nearly impossible to understand. As Meggs wrote, "According to newspaper reports, respectable and intelligent businessmen were unable to comprehend the lettering on these posters, yet they communicated well enough to fill auditoriums with a younger generation who deciphered, rather than read, the message."[25]

By the late 1960s, graphics such as those on San Francisco's psychedelic posters had spread across American consumer culture. Similar images were seen on buttons, bumper stickers, clothing, cars, countless record albums, and even ads in mainstream media. Meanwhile, in New York, designer Milton Glaser was putting his own spin on the counterculture graphics revolt at his Push Pin Studio.

Push Pin's style went beyond the psychedelic, combining aspects of the arts and crafts, art nouveau, and art deco movements with contemporary typography and illustration. Glaser designed one of the most iconic images from the 1960s: the incredibly popular poster for the 1967 album Bob Dylan's Greatest Hits. The poster features a silhouette of Bob Dylan's face and head in black while portraying his hair in electric colors.

This poster for Bob Dylan's Greatest Hits *combined psychedelic colors with art nouveau–style lines.*

The Influence of Punk Rock

Graphic styles inspired by the 1960s are still popular, especially in the world of fashion. Skate and surf-wear companies produce shoes, shirts, dresses, and skateboards with designs that would have been fashionable in the 1960s. Many of these have been blended with punk rock elements—a style of music, fashion, and art that arose in the mid-1970s. Punk rock eventually came to describe an attitude of rebelling against current societal trends, including rejecting racism, fascism, and capitalism. According to Greg Graffin, a singer-songwriter with the band Bad Religion,

> *Punk is: the personal expression of uniqueness that comes from the experiences of growing up in touch with our human ability to reason and ask questions; a movement that serves to refute social attitudes that have been perpetuated through willful ignorance of human nature; a process of questioning and commitment to understanding that results in self-progress, and through repetition, flowers into social evolution; a belief that this world is what we make of it, truth comes from our understanding of the way things are, not from the blind adherence to prescriptions about the way things should be; the constant struggle against fear of social repercussions.*[26]

Due to this attitude of rebellion, posters for punk rock bands were not meant to look conventionally beautiful, the way previous styles were. Instead, punk design focused on being different and authentic—not pretending to be a certain way for the sake of blending in. The fonts were mainly handwritten or designed to look like they had been cut out of magazines or newspapers, and the graphics had an intentionally posterized effect. The goal of punk rock posters was to completely depart from previous styles.

Punk rock was more a style of music and fashion than art, but artists were inspired by the unconventional design of punk music posters. In 2008, Shepard Fairey designed an iconic political poster that became instantly recognizable: the red, white, and blue *Hope* poster, which was created for Barack Obama's first presidential campaign. Like the Uncle Sam poster, it has been widely parodied. Some of the parodies are political, such as one showing George W. Bush with the caption, "Dope." Others refer to popular culture, such as a picture of Luke Skywalker with the caption, "A New Hope."

Because of the success of his original design, Fairey has created other posters in the same style, including one of a Muslim woman wearing an American flag as a hijab, with the caption, "We the People Are Greater than Fear." He said the images he created were inspired by his punk rock

Shepard Fairey is famous for the poster he created to advertise Barack Obama's first presidential campaign.

background, which can be seen in the posterization of the colors as well as the idea behind the images: "When the status quo is fearful and scapegoating, then the most punk rock you can be is finding common ground with your fellow human beings."[27]

Design in Advertising

Advertisements are so ingrained in Western culture that there are hardly any places where they cannot be seen. According to design company Canva, "research suggests we are exposed to, on average, 362 ads per day … but only 3 [percent] of these will make an impression."[28] In other words, people only remember about 12 of the ads they see each day. To make their ads stand out, designers must be clever and think outside the box, creating things people are not used to seeing.

In the mid-1800s, advertising became a big business when the first company dedicated entirely to designing ads was created; previously, companies had hired individual designers to make ads for them. This is still sometimes done today, and designers who do not work for any particular company are called freelancers. In today's job market, freelancers typically have more creative freedom and the ability to choose which projects they want to take on. However, they must work hard to remain competitive with large agencies, which employ many designers and often have more resources available to them. Additionally, they may have difficulty getting paid fairly for their work. Clients sometimes undervalue the effort graphic designers put into their designs, so they may offer too little money or no money at all. Designers who work for a firm do not have to negotiate prices for themselves; the company does it for them.

Magazines' Influence on Culture

Before television and the Internet, magazines played a major role in shaping society and culture. From the cover to the last page, the magazine influenced public opinion, promoted shared ideals, and helped people understand the world around them.

From the 1890s through the 1960s, when magazines experienced their greatest popularity, cover illustrations had the power to produce national icons. For example, the Gibson Girl illustrations created one of the earliest national standards for feminine beauty in the United States. These illustrations of full-figured women with thin waists, created by Charles Dana Gibson, first appeared on the cover of *LIFE* magazine in the 1890s. This set off a 20-year fad of Gibson Girls appearing on dishes, ashtrays, pillow covers, fans, and tablecloths as well as magazine covers.

Norman Rockwell was another enormously influential illustrator. His idealized pictures of daily life in America appeared on the covers of *The Saturday Evening Post* for more than 50 years. They did not show American life as it really was, but as Rockwell wanted it to be. His enduring popularity shows that many other people shared Rockwell's vision of what life should be like.

Beyond their cultural influence, magazines served as showcases for the most fashionable artistic concepts and trends in graphic design. Whether it was art nouveau in the 1890s, art deco in the 1920s, or modernism in postwar years, these styles of visual communication reached their widest audience in magazine layouts and advertisements.

Advertising Becomes a Business

By the mid-19th century, the Industrial Revolution had been churning out consumer goods for a generation. Where there had once been a lack of mass-produced clothes, canned food, health remedies, and tools, there were now too many of these products. This created intense competition among manufacturers. Companies that never had to advertise before were now forced to use aggressive sales techniques to reach consumers. This resulted in Volney Palmer founding the first advertising business in Philadelphia, Pennsylvania, in 1841.

Palmer was an ad broker; he bought ad space for companies in newspapers. N.W. Ayer opened the world's first full-service ad agency in Philadelphia in 1869. Ayer had a creative staff for planning and executing ad campaigns. Professional art editors hired illustrators to supervise the layouts of ads. The completed ads were then turned over to workers who specialized in ad placement in various publications.

MORTON® SALT
HOUSEHOLD
HINT #14
See copy on
side panel

MORTON®
SALT

THIS SALT DOES NOT SUPPLY ~~IODIDE, A NECESSARY NUTRIENT.~~

The Ayer ad agency created
the logo and slogan that
Morton Salt still uses today.

NET WT. 26 OZ. (1 LB.)

The Ayer ad agency operated successfully until 2002. It is widely known for its famous advertising slogans, including "When it rains it pours" for Morton Salt (1914), "I'd walk a mile for a Camel" for R.J. Reynolds Tobacco (1921), and "A diamond is forever" for De Beers (1948).

The Partnership of Magazines and Ads

Advertising agencies needed to reach the widest audience with their campaigns, and by 1880, there were more than 2,600 different magazines in the United States alone. While there was a high failure rate for magazines, several became national icons in the first decades of the 20th century, including *Vogue*, *Vanity Fair*, *Harper's Weekly*, *House and Garden*, *Ladies' Home Journal*, and *The Saturday Evening Post*. These and other magazines attracted astounding sums of money from advertisers.

Ad agencies fought to place larger ads than their competitors in the most popular magazines. This forced the periodicals to hire their own ad managers and art directors to make sense from the chaos. A good example is *Ladies' Home Journal*, where the pages were a jumble of opposing ads until graphic designer John Adams Thayer was hired in 1892 to clean up the visuals. According to the magazine's typographer, Frank Presby,

Thayer made up a set of rules for the Ladies' Home Journal *advertising columns that changed them from the ugly black mess produced by the desire of every advertiser to outdo all others and gave them instead an appearance pleasing to the eye. Illustration was likewise censored into a more artistic appearance. The aspect of the whole periodical was changed.*[29]

Changes in Printing

The techniques pioneered by Thayer gave rise to new, sophisticated standards of graphic representation. His work was aided by advances in halftone printing technology, which led magazines to switch from muddy, engraved illustrations to crisp, clean photographs. Journalism professors Sammye Johnson and Patricia Prijatel explained the benefits of photography, or halftones, in graphic design:

More and more magazines began using halftones to embellish articles. McClure's, *for example, included photographs from the lives of famous men in its "Human Document" series, while* Munsey's *used the nude female to illustrate a department titled "Artists and Their Work." Photos were still black and white, yet the images were nonetheless dramatic.* Collier's *news photographs of the 1898 Spanish-American War established the publication as the premier picture magazine of the time.*[30]

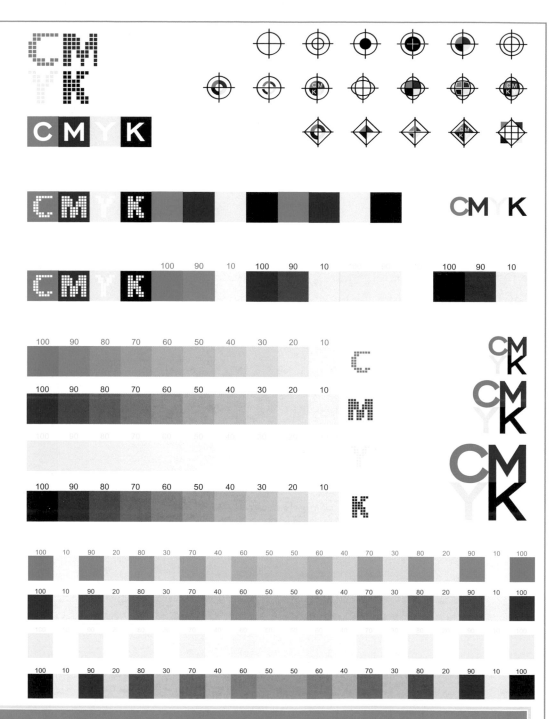

The change to photos saved publishers large amounts of money. A halftone reproduction cost about $20, whereas the price of an engraved illustration was about $300. The halftone process also allowed publishers to print in full color without the time and expense of lithography.

Because color photo film was not yet invented, color illustrations were shot as halftones. In what is known as process color, an illustration is photographically "separated" into three colors (cyan, magenta, and yellow) plus black. Each color is reproduced on a separate printing plate, and the tiny dots from each plate are lined up, or registered, so as to give a near-perfect reproduction of an illustration, with all the variety of tones and colors.

Process color allowed magazines to print pictures by renowned illustrators such as Maxfield Parrish, whose stunning work was featured on the covers of *Collier's*, *Ladies' Home Journal*, and other magazines. These illustrations were printed in a style called poster cover, which had no lines or type in the picture to detract from the beauty. Poster cover magazines were often framed and hung in people's homes.

Photojournalism

Until the 1930s, high-quality illustrations and photographs were used as adjuncts to magazine stories—they provided visuals to highlight the words in the articles. However, that concept changed when Henry Luce, the powerful American publisher and editor of *TIME*, bought *LIFE* magazine in 1936. Luce believed many Americans were undereducated and sought a new way to bring them the latest science news, current events, and human-interest stories. To do so, he hired the best photographers in the business to tell stories a new way, through photojournalism—using photographs rather than words to convey the news.

Selling a Lifestyle

When designers work with a company, they are trying to help the company figure out the best way to make its products look good. The company will consult with the graphic artist about how to design the product and the ads to make them as appealing as possible to consumers. For instance, a successful campaign for Coca-Cola involved creating bottles with people's names on them, and their ads for those bottles encourage people to share a Coke with a friend. When people spot their friend's name on a bottle, they may be more likely to buy Coke because it feels more personal to them. In this way, Coca-Cola promotes its product based more on the idea of a strong friendship than on the quality of its product.

LIFE was printed in a large format on heavy white paper. The first issue featured a new type of graphic design. It contained 50 pages of pictures with short captions of text accompanying the photos. Although Luce only printed 380,000 copies of the first issue, within 4 months, *LIFE* was selling more than 1 million copies a week. The new magazine format could not be ignored by publishers, and it did not take long for others, including *Look*, the Paris *Match*, and the British *Picture Post* to imitate *LIFE*. These magazines created what was called a visual literacy among the public. People learned to spot good images and came to expect more than simple photos and articles in their magazines. As Luce noted, "To see life; to see the world; to eyewitness great events; to see strange things … to see man's work … to see and be amazed … to see and be shown is now the will and expectancy of half of mankind."[31]

Uniting Text and Pictures

The magazine art directors in the 1950s and 1960s belonged to what was called the New York style of design. Practitioners of the New York style were editorial and advertising designers who took the separate units of text, photos, and illustrations and unified them into single visual statements.

At *McCall's*, art director and photographer Otto Storch linked type and photography in unique ways. For example, in an article titled "Why Mommy Can't Read," the words are written on a pair of glasses, but look bent and wavy, as if distorted by failing vision. For the article "The Forty-Winks Reducing Plan," a woman is shown sleeping on her side on a mattress made of type. Her body causes sags in the mattress, and the text of the article follows the curves of her body. Commenting on such novel ideas, Storch wrote in 1980, "I did not think that pictures and typography were an end in themselves, but just component parts of the message … For me, idea, copy, art and typography became inseparable."[32]

In addition to articles, the New York style was seen in the advertisements that filled magazine pages. Gene Federico was one of the premiere advertising art directors and designers in the post–World War II era, recognized for his ability to push the boundaries of ad design. Federico's specialty was typography. For example, a 1953 ad for *Woman's Day* shows a woman riding a bicycle. The wheels of the bike are two lowercase o's in the Futura font that are part of the words "Go Out" in the headline "She's Got to Go Out to Get *Woman's Day*."

Commenting on Federico's style, Steven Heller wrote in the *New York Times*,

At most agencies, copywriters dominated the creative side, with text segregated from images in unimaginative, cookie-cutter layouts. The

art director was a mere functionary … Federico, however … became one of a handful of contemporary advertising designers to develop a distinctly [modern] approach to graphic design. It emphasized clean layout, asymmetrical composition and sans-serif typefaces, and it was rooted in the often witty union of word and picture.[33]

Humor in Advertising

Federico was one of the first people to believe that humor could be used to sell a product. Today, with so many funny or clever ads, it may be hard to understand that at one time, advertisers did not like to associate their products with humor. That changed in the 1960s, when legendary advertising agency Doyle Dane Bernbach began taking what was called the concept approach to advertising.

Concept advertisers used memorable phrases that were repeated in ads with different pictures, often with humorous results. For example, Doyle Dane Bernbach's first successful campaign for Levy's Rye Bread showed the words "You don't have to be Jewish to love Levy's" in a simple font. The words were placed with photos of various people, including an older Native American person, an African American man, and a young Japanese boy all enjoying sandwiches on Levy's bread. Created by writer Judy Protas and art director Bill Taubin,

the ads were an international hit and dramatically increased the sales of Levy's rye.

Other Doyle Dane Bernbach ads became cultural milestones in the 1960s. The "Think Small" ads for the Volkswagen Beetle used graphic design to make a point. A small image of the VW was placed on the upper left corner of the page surrounded by a sea of white paper. Beneath, the words "Think Small" and some clever copy conveyed a simple yet eye-catching and humorous message.

Many of the agency's daring designs are attributed to its founder, William Bernbach, who summarized his design philosophies with two memorable statements: "Rules are what the artist breaks; the memorable never emerged from a formula," and "Logic and over-analysis can immobilize and sterilize an idea. It's like love—the more you analyze it, the faster it disappears."[34]

Despite Bernbach's words, many business executives were analyzing ads and reaching the same conclusion: Good design can sell products. Advertisers sought to create total saturation for their products, putting their logos on nearly everything. As a result, advertisements showed up everywhere in the decades that followed. In addition to their usual place on TV and radio, ads popped up on bus stops, automobiles, billboards, signboards, the walls of public restrooms, and even on T-shirts and caps bearing logos for designers.

Ads are everywhere in today's society, especially in big cities.

By the mid-1990s, the average American consumer living in a typical city was looking at more than 3,000 commercial messages each day, counting logos on products. This was a result of more than $148 billion spent annually by the ad industry. Marketers increasingly aimed their ad campaigns at young people, and consumer spending continued to rise throughout the decade and into the 21st century.

Building Trust

In recent years, the goal of advertisers has moved away from selling specific items and toward creating a sense

Advertising Tricks

There are several well-known tricks advertisers use to get people to notice their products. The Federal Trade Commission (FTC), a government agency that protects customers from unfair business practices, lists several:

- *Association: Using images (like a cartoon character or the American flag), in the hope you'll transfer your good feelings about the image to the product.*

- *Call to action: Telling you what to do—"Buy today!" or "Vote now"—removes all doubt about next steps ...*

- *Hype: Using words like amazing and incredible make products seem really exciting.*

- *Must-have: Suggesting that you must have the product to be happy, popular, or satisfied.*

- *Fear: Using a product to solve something you worry about, like bad breath.[1]*

Using certain colors or fonts can also change the way a person thinks about a product. For instance, according to *Business Insider*, a 2002 study "measured how a webpage's background influenced consumers looking to buy a car. When the background was green with pennies on it, customers spent more time [looking at] the cost info, but when the background was red with flames, they spent more time looking at the safety section."[2]

1. "It's All About the Technique," Federal Trade Commission, July 2013. www.consumer.ftc.gov/articles/0375-its-all-about-technique.
2. Tanya Lewis, "9 Sneaky Psychology Tricks Companies Use to Get You to Buy Stuff," *Business Insider*, February 10, 2016. www.businessinsider.com/9-sneaky-psychology-tricks-companies-use-to-get-you-to-buy-stuff-2016-2.

of brand loyalty in their consumers. Companies want people to trust their name and buy the products they make. In the past, when advertising was new, people tended to trust the ads they saw. However, as time went on, people realized that ads often inflated the truth to sell their product, so they stopped believing many of the ads they saw. For this reason, instead of coming up with slogans about a product, many ads feature slogans about the company. For instance, the slogan of Jif peanut butter is, "Choosy moms choose Jif." This slogan does not make a claim about the taste of the peanut butter; instead, it creates the idea in a consumer's mind that any Jif product is better than the competitor's. By doing this, companies hope their customers will spread the word to their friends.

In a society where technology and the Internet are increasingly present in people's lives, some advertisers are trying to make their brand seem cool by using Internet memes in their ads. In one instance, Virgin Media used "Success Kid"—the image of a young boy who appears to be celebrating a victory with a fist pump—on their billboards. The picture is accompanied by the words, "Tim just realised his parents get HD channels at no extra cost." This statement shows a change in marketing strategy: Rather than trying to get people to use Virgin Media because it is better than its competitors, the company is trying to create the idea in the consumer's mind that

their service solves a problem the customer has—in this case, how to get something the customer wants for less money than they would normally pay.

Another campaign that took inspiration from social media was a 2015 multimedia campaign by the Partnership for Drug-Free Kids. Rather than trying to sell something, the organization used hashtags and emojis to connect with young adults to convince them not to do drugs or drink alcohol. The campaign, which is called #WeGotYou, features "[i]ndividual emoji sentences ... [that] act as cryptic messages, encouraging teens to 'crack the code' via the unique URL featured at the end of each ad."[35] The ads can be seen on billboards and online, and there is a mobile-only website where young adults can find the answers to these emoji sentences and submit their own.

Other companies have changed their marketing strategy in more radical ways. Patagonia, a company that makes outdoor clothing and sporting gear, has run several "anti-ads" that encourage people to think harder about their purchases. One of the most famous shows the words "DON'T BUY THIS JACKET" in large black letters on top of a picture of a Patagonia jacket. To the right, the ad explains the Common Threads Initiative—a project to reduce the amount of waste generated by consumers. With the Common Threads Initiative, Patagonia encourages consumers to only buy what they need, to send their damaged clothing back to Patagonia to be fixed at no extra cost, and to pass on their clothing to others or return it to Patagonia when they no longer need it. The website Tint explained why this was a clever marketing move:

Firstly, it creates a loyal audience because their primary aim is making sure their customers are happy—not selling more products.

Secondly, it builds trust.

Think about it logically: if a brand is encouraging you to send back a product if it's broken, you're more likely to think it won't break, because why the heck would they promise to do that if they're selling a shoddy product?[36]

The ad was eye-catching not only because of the message, but also because of the design, with large letters that stood out clearly against the blue jacket and gray background.

The Anti-Ad Movement

The increasing number of ads over the years created a backlash among those who were tired of being bombarded by ads everywhere they went. In Vancouver, Canada, former advertisers Kalle Lasn and Bill Schmalz were so fed up with corporate ads that they founded *Adbusters* magazine to refute the claims made by advertisers. According to Lasn, "Since the second world war we have created a consumer culture pumping something like 3,000 to 5,000 messages into our brains every day from the time you are a baby."[37] Lasn believed that this bombardment prevented people from thinking about the negative costs of consumer culture. For example, some of the most expensive designer brands are made by Chinese laborers in sweatshops where the working conditions border on slavery. In addition, there are dozens of environmental problems with mass-consumerism that add to global warming, air and water pollution, and depletion of natural resources.

To educate young consumers, *Adbusters* used clever graphic designs to wage anticonsumer campaigns. These ads were called anti-ads, uncommercials, or subvertisements (subversive advertisements) and were created for culture jamming—opposing the corporate advertising that dominates modern society. For example, *Adbusters* created spoof ads that looked like the expensive advertisements created for Marlboro, Calvin Klein, Apple, McDonald's, and others. One example showed a man having an operation in the background. In the foreground, a hospital heart monitor displayed the McDonald's logo and the words, "Big Mac Attack!" Another showed a Nike sneaker divided in half with a white chalk line. On the toe it said, "Nike $250," while on the heel, it said, "Sweatshop 83¢." This illustrated the difference between the huge profit Nike makes and the small salary it pays the workers who make the shoes.

Adbusters also waged a battle against consumerism with campaigns such as TV Turnoff Week and Buy Nothing Day. The poster for the November 2007 Buy Nothing campaign featured a red frame with the word "Celebrate" on top. Large block letters in boxes of black and white said "BUY NOTHING DAY." The A in DAY was the uncapped pyramid with the all-seeing eye featured on the back of the $1 bill.

The Buy Nothing campaign generated media attention and some controversy. MTV refused to run an *Adbusters* commercial featuring another piece of graphics wizardry—a giant animated clay pig emerging from a map of North America. Despite the problems, *Adbusters* estimated that at least half a million people participated in the campaign and bought nothing that day.

The minds behind the anti-advertising campaigns have won a substantial number of awards for their graphic arts designs. The magazine was known for its design, which shocked readers through juxtaposition, or contrast between two elements, such as in the McDonald's spoof.

Getting Creative

Although magazines were an important part of the rise of advertising, increased use of technology has made it difficult for print magazines to stay in business. In the last decade, many magazines have either stopped publishing print issues or reduced the number of magazines they publish. Ads are moving online, but the invention of ad-blocking programs means fewer people are seeing them. For this reason, some people argue that print magazines can still be good for advertisers. According to Britt Fero, executive vice president and head of strategy for the Seattle office of the ad agency Publicis, "Just buying [a magazine] or getting it in the mail provokes the reader to engage in a way that digital doesn't. If you have time to read a magazine, then you're going to really engage with the ads in there. Print ads should inspire you to look at them even longer."[38] This has led to more creative ads that make the consumer take a second look. For instance, an ad for the World Wildlife Federation has two pictures side by side. The left picture shows a shark fin emerging from the water with the caption, "Horrifying." The right picture shows only water with the caption, "More horrifying." It may take the viewer a moment to understand that the point of the ad is to draw attention to the disappearance of sharks caused by humans, but that moment spent looking at the ad makes the message stick in the viewer's mind.

Print magazines are still popular with certain people, but it is true that they have been overshadowed by online media. This does not mean graphic design is unnecessary; in fact, the opposite is true. The Internet has created the field of web design, and new software gives graphic designers more flexibility than ever before.

Print magazines are still popular with some people, but nearly all of the magazines that are still in circulation also publish their articles online.

CHAPTER
FIVE

Modern Design

Throughout most of history, graphic designers were mainly concerned with making sure their message was communicated clearly and efficiently. They were concerned with which typefaces were the easiest to read and how to use design elements in a way that would have the most impact on the viewer.

However, by the early 1970s, the clean, modernist approach began to break down when young designers rejected the rational communication style of mainstream art directors. The new generation, raised during the psychedelic 1960s, sought to put their own individual stamp on designs, rather than stick to established rules. This signaled the beginning of what art historians call the postmodern or new-wave era. As R. Roger Remington explained in *American Modernism: Graphic Design, 1920–1960,* "Designers questioned the need for functionality in graphic design. They preferred solutions that most often were personal expressions involving complexity, subjectivity, and ambiguity."[39]

Subjectivity, or interpreting something based on personal opinions, was not an option available to earlier graphic designers. Nor was ambiguity, or expressing something in a vague or uncertain way. However, there were several factors at work that made artists turn away from modernist design in the 1970s. It was an era when women, people of color, and immigrants were playing a more essential role in advertising and design for the first time. The newcomers challenged the way things were done while at the same time introducing fresh sensibilities and creativity to a field that had largely been dominated by white males.

Another change shook graphics tradition in the mid-1970s, when punk became popular. Punk graphic artists created fanzines, or 'zines for short, which were homemade music magazines about popular punk bands. The 'zines used scribbled words, crude drawings, and letters and pictures torn out of popular magazines—what Richard Hollis called "anti-Design."[40] In an era before personal computers, punks reproduced 'zines with lithography and photocopy machines.

What Is Postmodernism?

The last quarter of the 20th century is known as the postmodern era. In *A History of Graphic Design*, communications professor Philip B. Meggs explained postmodernism and the motivating forces behind it:

By the 1970s, many people believed the modern era was drawing to a close in art, design, politics, and literature. The cultural norms of Western society were scrutinized and the authority of traditional institutions was questioned. An era of pluralism emerged as people began to dispute the underlying tenets of modernism. The continuing quest for equality by women and minorities contributed to a growing climate of cultural diversity, as did immigration, international travel, and global communications. Accepted viewpoints were challenged by those who sought to remedy bias, prejudice, and distortion in the historical record. The social, economic, and environmental awareness of the period caused many to believe the modern aesthetic was no longer relevant in an emerging postindustrial society. People in many fields—including architects, economists, feminists, and even theologians—embraced the term postmodernism to express a climate of cultural change. Maddeningly vague and overused, postmodernism became a byword in the last quarter of the twentieth century.

In design, postmodernism designated the work of architects and designers who were breaking with the international style so prevalent since the [1930s]. Postmodernism sent shock waves through the design establishment as it challenged the order and clarity of modern design, particularly corporate design ... Perhaps the international style had been so thoroughly refined, explored, and accepted that a backlash was inevitable.[1]

1. Philip B. Meggs, *A History of Graphic Design*. New York, NY: Wiley, 1998, p. 432.

Breaking the Old Rules

The rise of 'zines was aided by technology that gave graphic artists greater control over the production process. The photomechanical transfer, or PMT, camera is a large machine that looks like a giant enlarger and is used in photography darkrooms. The machine, introduced around 1970, transfers photographs, illustrations, or type into high-contrast black-and-white reproductions called photostats. It can also be used to enlarge or reduce images to fit into layouts. With PMTs, graphic artists could produce complete finished layouts, or camera-ready art, instead of giving detailed instructions to typesetters and halftone makers. In this way, the PMT process allowed the new generation of designers to put their personal stamp on each and every layout.

While most graphic artists used PMTs to produce clean layouts, German-born designer Wolfgang Weingart went to extremes in Switzerland. Feeling that the refined modernist style had become boring, Weingart began challenging accepted design rules in the late 1960s. By the mid-1970s, he had helped create the new-wave style, which abandoned stark, organized modernism in favor of wide letter spacing and the tendency to change fonts, sizes, and letter weights (such as bold or narrow) in a single word. This style was combined with collages in which Weingart created a single layout with photographs, photographic negatives, overlapping images, numbers, arrows, boxes of type, and cartoon balloons filled with words.

Terry Jones, a former editor of *Vogue*, followed a similar path in 1980 with his 'zine *i-D*. According to Hollis, the magazine "was the most energetic expression of every kind of new technology, which it used by abusing it—enormously enlarged photocopies and copies distorted by moving the paper, Polaroid instant photographs over- or under-exposed and scratched or painted on."[41]

A Technological Revolution

Soon after Jones created his punk magazine, designers had new tools at their disposal. Digital word processing programs were first introduced in the late 1970s, but the digital revolution in graphics did not begin until Apple introduced its Macintosh computer in 1984. This machine allowed designers, for the first time, to create numerous type fonts in various sizes and manipulate and organize text, photos, and images on a computer monitor.

The fonts and icons used on the early Macs were created by designer Susan Kare and were used on computers for years. Kare invented the "command" symbol on Mac keyboards. She also created a hand icon that pushed pages up and down, a suitcase to represent the document folder, the trash can icon, and a bomb with a lit fuse that appeared when the computer crashed. In addition, Kare designed the tool icons called

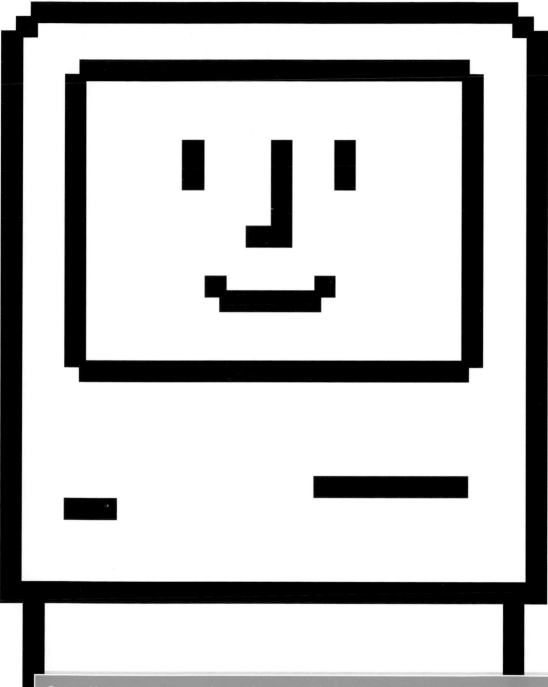

Susan Kare created many icons that are still used on computers today, although the style has been updated. This icon represented the Apple computer.

the Lasso, the Grabber, and the Paint Bucket for the first painting and illustration software programs, MacPaint and MacDraw.

Kare had to ensure that her icons would be understood by people on every continent. The earliest Mac operating systems were only 400 KB in size—a modern 3-minute MP3 file is more than 10 times bigger. Therefore, Kare's designs had to use very few pixels, which are the dots on the screen that generate images. To help her achieve this task, Kare studied ancient mosaics, pictures made of small pieces of colored tile or glass.

Some of Kare's designs were retired when Apple created OS X (operating system 10) in 2000. However, according to the Museum of Modern Art in New York, Kare remains "a pioneering and influential computer iconographer ... Utilizing a minimalist grid of pixels and constructed with mosaic-like precision, her icons communicate their function immediately and memorably, with wit and style."[42]

California New Wave

The introduction of the computer sent shock waves through the graphic arts world. As the American Institute of Graphic Arts website states, "Most designers were skeptical of—if not completely opposed to—the idea of integrating the computer into design

Revolutionary Software

The introduction of Macintosh computers in 1984 changed graphic design forever. The machines were developed with the needs of artists in mind, and several types of early Macintosh software revolutionized visual communication. One of the earliest programs, MacPaint, created by computer programmer Bill Atkinson and graphic designer Susan Kare, had a groundbreaking human interface in which the tool icons controlled by the newly invented mouse or graphics tablet enabled designers to digitize their ideas easily and naturally.

In 1985, Macintosh began selling its computers with Adobe PostScript. This software sent text, images, and graphic elements to the Apple LaserWriter printer. Another piece of software, Aldus PageMaker, allowed graphic artists to pick fonts, type sizes, page margins, borders, and other elements.

Together with the Macintosh computer, the software created a new field called desktop publishing, or DTP. People could now combine text and images on a computer for use in publishing books, magazines, advertisements, and creative projects. This saved a great deal of money and time for those who worked to prepare pages for printing. Today, desktop publishing is a multibillion-dollar business, and nearly every graphic artist uses a computer for visual communications.

practice, perhaps fearing an uncertain future wherein the tactility [sensitivity] of the hand was usurped [taken over] by the mechanics of bits and bytes."[43] However, with a computer's ability to integrate graphic design, typesetting, photo reproduction, and printing functions, most designers could not ignore the new technology. Design schools were required to change their curricula, and art directors were forced to learn to work with unfamiliar and often unpredictable machines.

Designers such as April Greiman were able to use this new tool in ways that changed the visual design world forever. Los Angeles-based Greiman was one of the first graphic artists to recognize the potential of the early Macs. Having studied with Weingart, she experimented with ways to bring a new-wave sensibility to a digital format. Her first attempt, a poster called *Iris Light*, was created when Greiman shot a traditional film photograph of an image on a video monitor. Discussing the piece that was a hybrid of old and new technologies, Greiman said of the image, "Instead of looking like a bad photograph, the image ... looked like a painting; it captured the spirit of light."[44]

Greiman found new ways to incorporate unusual digital techniques in 1986 when she was asked to contribute to an issue of *Design Quarterly*. Upon taking the assignment, Greiman understood that it was the responsibility of a postmodern designer to question accepted concepts. In her contribution, she challenged the idea of what a magazine is supposed to be, as the title of the project, *Does It Make Sense?*, suggests. Although she was commissioned to create 32 pages of designs, Greiman discarded the notion of a typical magazine layout. Instead, *Does It Make Sense?* was a pullout poster that was nearly 3 by 6 feet (0.9 by 1.8 m). The image on the poster was a digital collage of Greiman's body overlaid with low-resolution images of a dinosaur, the earth from the surface of the moon, and random text and drawings. An article about Greiman on the American Institute of Graphic Arts website described the difficulty of creating this work with an early computer:

The process of integrating digitized video images and [computerized] type was not unlike pulling teeth in the early days of Macintosh and MacDraw. The files were so large, and the equipment so slow that she would send the file to print when she left the studio in the evening and it would just be finished when she returned in the morning.[45]

Greiman also used MacDraw to cut and paste various parts of her body, demonstrating some largely unrecognized abilities of digital equipment. Her poster was controversial at the time, and her style came to be known as California new wave. Today, such images are seen everywhere in advertisements, video graphics, and magazine articles.

The invention of the Macintosh computer revolutionized graphic design. Today, the majority of design projects are done on computers.

Emoji Design

Ever since the first chat programs were created, people have found that the things they write are sometimes misinterpreted because people rely heavily on tone of voice to interpret a statement. To clarify things, people began using emoticons. These were simple text combinations such as :) for a happy face and :(for a sad face. In Western culture, the eyes often remained the same and the symbol used for the mouth was changed to represent emotion. In Eastern cultures, the symbol for a happy face might be ^_^ and the symbol for a sad face might be ;_; because the eyes were used to show emotion instead of the mouth.

In 1999, Shigetaka Kurita, a Japanese researcher, created the first emojis—the pictures users see today on their cell phones and other devices. According to Creative Market,

> Behind every picture is a unique numeric value defined in an international encoding standard known as Unicode. That's how a lollipop becomes U+1F36D … What that means for designers is that they have some freedom to decide what picture best represents that standard number. Of course there are some guidelines, but there is also wide creative freedom … Google's Android, Apple's iOS, Microsoft's Windows, Facebook and Twitter, have all reinterpreted the original alphabet adding their own aesthetic touch.[1]

1. Laura Busche, "Meet the Graphic Designers Behind the Emojis We Love," Creative Market, May 2, 2016. creativemarket.com/blog/meet-the-graphic-designers-behind-the-emojis-we-love.

In later years, Greiman continued to make lasting contributions to the world of graphic design. Her posters such as the 1989 *Pacific Wave, Fortuny Museum*, the 1993 *AIGA Communication Graphics*, and the 2004 *Cal State Sacramento— Think About What You Think About* are outstanding examples of postmodern visual communication. Greiman also challenged accepted forms of language. In 1984, when CalArts invited her to direct its graphic design program, she changed the department name to Visual Communications. Like earlier methods of production, Greiman felt that the term "graphic design" was too limiting for this exciting field.

Emphasizing Form Over Function

Advances in software and digital technology continued to expand the abilities of graphic artists throughout the late 1980s. For example, the page-design application QuarkXPress, first introduced in 1987, allowed designers to place elements on a page with new precision and accuracy. This software was soon in widespread use by graphic artists, page designers, typesetters, and printers.

In the early 1990s, David Carson used this software, which was advanced at the time, to astonish the design community with a new breed of magazine that was as original as it was unreadable. Carson, a former professional surfer, became a graphic designer in the late 1980s. As the art director for *Beach Culture*, *Surfer*, and *Ray Gun* between 1989 and 1996, Carson discarded magazine design rules in which text and images were laid out in a traditional grid pattern of columns, margins, and photo borders. Instead, he favored unlimited visual expression in the form of upside-down or backward type, wavy lines of text that might slump off the bottom of the page, several type fonts within a single paragraph, and sentences completely obscured with illustrations or other sentences laid over them in a different color. Letters could be sliced off, and sentences might be incomplete, which invited the reader to fill in his or her own ideas.

In one issue of *Beach Culture*, Carson created confusing, out-of-sequence page numbers that were larger than the headlines of the articles. In *Ray Gun*, he used single lines of text on a double page spread, extending across two pages. On another occasion, he ran two separate articles intermixed with one another to create a confusing jumble that required extreme patience from the reader trying to make sense of the words.

Carson was also famous for his odd photographic reproductions. A photo of country singer Lyle Lovett showed only his bare feet. For an issue featuring the Beastie Boys, the cover was left blank except for the top two inches, which displayed a photo of the group. Carson explained that this was the only part of the magazine that shoppers at a magazine stand would see anyway. Carson also printed humorous, weird, and bizarre photos and illustrations sent in by subscribers, eliminating the distance between professional and amateur designers. Like the text, these might be printed upside down, as negative images, or sliced and diced to fit into layouts. In *The End of Print: The Graphic Design of David Carson*, musician David Byrne of the band Talking Heads described Carson's extreme graphics as "beautiful, radical, impractical design of and by the people … hip as Rock & Roll."[46]

Oddly, although Carson is associated with the computer design revolution, many of his most innovative designs were created as traditional, old-style, camera-ready art laid out on cardboard. Whatever the case, his groundbreaking work shook up the world of graphics. Although it was condemned by professionals, it was beloved by a younger generation raised not on magazines but on the wild images of music videos.

The Creation of New Fonts

While Carson's work was on the cutting edge of visual communication, a new generation of typographers began using computers to design typefaces. They created an explosion of new fonts in the early 1990s unmatched in graphic arts history.

At Adobe, calligrapher and mathematician Sumner Stone worked with Carol Twombly and Robert Slimbach to create the typographic program called Adobe Originals. These high-quality fonts, such as Utopia, Lithos, and Adobe's version of the classic Caslon, were used by desktop publishers in countless designs. Meanwhile, Apple designers created another version of Garamond, a narrower rendering of the serif typeface created in the 16th century. Apple used this font, called ITC Garamond, with its classic Apple corporate logo and with its popular 1997 "Think Different" advertising campaign. However, many typographers criticized Apple's ITC Garamond, calling it a poorly designed takeoff of the classic style and "Garamond" in name only. Despite the criticism, the font was seen by billions of people in the 1990s. In 2002, Apple took another font, Myriad, designed for Adobe by Slimbach and Twombly, and created its own version for advertising and packaging. Called Myriad Apple, the sans serif font was used on the early iPods and was also used to market them.

Beyond the major corporations, countless type designers were empowered by the computer to create their own studios, called type foundries, a term dating back to the early years of printing when type was forged from hot metal. Of the more successful type foundries, Emigre Graphics of Berkeley, California, was among the first to take advantage of the typographic potential of Macintosh computers in the mid-1980s. In an interview with British journalist Rhonda Rubinstein, Emigre founder Zuzana Licko described the unique possibilities she saw in the Mac:

> *The Macintosh … was a relatively crude tool back then, so established designers looked upon it as a cute novelty. But to me it seemed as wondrously uncharted as my fledgling design career. It was a fortunate coincidence; I'm sure that being free of preconceived notions regarding typeface design helped me in exploring this new medium to the fullest … It has continued to be the ideal tool for me.*[47]

In the years that followed, Licko and other Emigre designers created controversy with eccentric fonts such as Dead History, Exocet, Keedy Sans, Remedy, and Totally Gothic. Although some challenged the experimental look of the type, unusual Emigre fonts were seen in major advertising campaigns and publication designs. In addition,

COLD WATER CANYON

AMERICAN

Chromolithography

NATIONAL LEAGUE CHAMPIONSHIP SERIES

Northwest

Appalachian Blue Grass

ENVIRONMENTAL

SLIDING ALUMINUM DOORS

Agricultural

Yosemite National Park

INDIGENOUS SHRUBS OF SANTA MONICA

Emigre Graphics created unusual fonts such as Dead History, shown here.

the foundry published the graphic design magazine *Emigre* for 21 years, from 1984 to 2005.

Emigre was one of the first major publications produced on a Macintosh, and its innovative and outspoken articles were extremely influential within the visual communications industry. Describing the antimodernist style of the magazine, Steven Heller and Seymour Chwast wrote in *Graphic Style: From Victorian to Digital,*

> The tabloid-sized quarterly defied the tenets of Modern layout much in the same way that sixties Psychedelic poster artists upended the rules of legibility—laying down rules of their own. Under Modernism, type had become a neutral frame within which crisp and clean photographs or abstract illustrations were composed. Emigre *was typocentric. Its typography was its content. By eradicating any semblance of the Modernist grid,* [Emigre *magazine founder Rudy*] *VanderLans opened up the printed page to unfettered, raucously artful typographic configurations.*[48]

The art seen in *Emigre* pushed the boundaries of accepted ideas about graphic arts. However, in the big money world of advertising, corporations still needed their ads to clearly sell products even while they projected a hip, cool image. This resulted in advertising designs Heller and Chwast

described as "controlled chaos."[49] The ads incorporated some of the unusual techniques pioneered by Emigre and Carson, such as oddly cropped photos and mixed font sizes and styles. However, the layouts remained readable enough to convey the advertiser's message, which not only sold a product, but also tried to present the corporation as sharing common values with the young, cutting-edge MTV generation.

Design Online

Even as art directors were redrawing the rule books, graphic design entered a new era with the advent of the Internet. Although it is difficult for many to remember today, the general public barely knew of the Internet in 1993, when the Mosaic web browser was first introduced. However, beginning in 1994, public use of the World Wide Web doubled annually, leaving corporations scrambling to create their own websites. By 1997, new website addresses were being created at a rate of 1 per minute, and there were an estimated 150 million websites. That number had topped 1 billion by 2000.

Unlike books and magazines, websites incorporate not only text and images, but also sounds, video, and animation. Graphic artists who transformed into web designers could no longer think of making individual page layouts but had to create interconnected websites that incorporated pages that were connected by hyperlinks, which are often simply called links.

One of the challenges for graphic designers is creating websites that look good on devices of all sizes.

Designs could be three-dimensional, such as rotating cubes with information on each side, or they could be point-and-click websites where various parts of an image led to different web pages. Website design was only limited by imagination. Those schooled in the controlled chaos of the late 1980s and early 1990s had a natural advantage.

By 2000, the integration of motion graphics, animation, video feeds, and music into website design created a fusion between the traditional print media, broadcast television, and movies. This expansion added yet another dimension to graphic design that was unthinkable as recently as the early 1990s.

A parallel revolution has taken place outside of the world of professional designers. Software such as Adobe Dreamweaver, introduced in 1997, and companies such as GeoCities allowed amateurs to design their own complex, interactive websites. In more recent years, website development software has become extremely user-friendly. Today, nearly anyone with computer skills can create a website with services such as Squarespace and Wix. As a result, countless people have become Internet graphic designers. Their websites deliver stories, art, music, movies, product information, and educational materials to a worldwide audience.

The wide variety of backgrounds, fonts, animations, and other features was sometimes dazzling to these amateur website designers. Websites that were created in the 1990s often combined so many different elements that they were difficult to read and are generally considered to be ugly by today's standards. The British company Design Juices described this point in the evolution of web design:

> The mere fact that some websites were suddenly deemed "ugly" was an important development in web design. Even up to the late 1990s, simply having a website was a major selling point. Design elements that would be laughed off the web today were still perfectly acceptable before GeoCities made web publishing easy ... Web designers focused most of their attention on interaction between the website and user, and these interactivity principles are still alive and well today (unlike user-created GeoCities websites).[50]

Although unusual backgrounds and fonts can be fun and exciting to play with, they sometimes make websites difficult to read and navigate. This is why businesses hire graphic designers to make their websites look professional and give the user the best experience. Professionally designed websites look more trustworthy; someone is more likely to believe information they find on a nicely designed website than on one that looks homemade. A nice design does not automatically mean everything on the website is true, but it is one way businesses can create the idea of credibility, or trustworthiness, in their customers' minds.

When graphic designers create a website, they focus on making it easy to read and use while still making it look visually appealing. They try to keep the design simple, using only a few colors and fonts. They also try to make sure users can quickly find everything they are looking for. For this reason, most websites have adopted certain similar features. On many websites, for example, the links to different parts of the website are at the top of the page. This ensures that visitors do not have to hunt around a website; they know exactly where to go to find what they need. Although designers try to work within certain boundaries, they can let their creativity shine in the details of a website.

Looking Toward the Future

Just as Gutenberg's press brought communication to the masses in the 15th century, the Internet allows people from any region of the globe to reach out to a mass audience. Since the earliest inventions of art and language, graphic artists have played a major role in helping the human race in its quest for interaction and communication. Nearly everything people see today has an element of graphic design in it, and new areas are developing all the time. One article on *Fast Company's* design website listed some possible jobs future graphic designers might have, including:

- Augmented reality designer: As virtual reality becomes more popular, designers will be needed to create the worlds people are experiencing through their headsets.

- Avatar programmer: People who participate in virtual reality can use an avatar to represent themselves. Designers can create an avatar that looks as much like the real person as possible.

- Human organ designer: "We are very close to being able to reproduce artificial biologically fitted tissues ... The prospect of artificially made human organs is just around the corner. Who's going to design and fit these organs to their end user? Designers will be there, sooner or later."[51]

- Real-time 3-D designer: As 3-D technology continues to improve, it has possible uses beyond the entertainment world. Businesses and schools may one day use 3-D models to help them meet their goals, and they will need designers to help create those models.

These jobs sound futuristic, but in a world where technology is advancing all the time, they may one day become reality. However, even if they do, there will still be a need for graphic artists to continue designing books, websites, posters, advertisements, and more.

Notes

Chapter One:
Art in Everyday Life

1. United States Department of the Treasury, "FAQs: Currency." www.treasury.gov/resource-center/faqs/Currency/Pages/edu_faq_currency_portraits.aspx.

2. Herbert Bayer et al., *Seven Designers Look at Trademark Design*. Chicago, IL: Theobald, 1952, p. 50.

3. Quoted in Charlotte Jirousek, "The Arts and Crafts Movement," Art, Design, and Visual Thinking, 1995. char.txa.cornell.edu/art/decart/artcraft/artcraft.htm.

4. Jeremy Aynsley, *A Century of Graphic Design*. Hauppauge, NY: Barron's Educational Series, 2001, p. 16.

5. Aynsley, *A Century of Graphic Design*, p. 16.

6. Quoted in "About: Biography," The Father of Industrial Design: Raymond Loewy. www.raymondloewy.com/about.html#biography.

7. Quoted in "About: Biography," The Father of Industrial Design: Raymond Loewy.

Chapter Two:
Design in Books

8. Norma Levarie, *The Art and History of Books*. Newcastle, DE: Oak Knoll, 1995, p. 60.

9. Quoted in BBC, "Documentary Description," *The Medieval Mind: The Machine That Made Us*, Cosmo Learning, 2010. cosmolearning.org/documentaries/the-medieval-mind-the-machine-that-made-us-2008/1/.

10. Quoted in Nicole Howard, *The Book: The Life Story of a Technology*. Westport, CT: Greenwood, 2005, p. 32.

11. Quoted in Michel Wlassikoff, *The Story of Graphic Design in France*. Corte Madre, CA: Gingko, 2005, p. 17.

12. Quoted in Richard Hollis, *Graphic Design: A Concise History*. London, UK: Thames & Hudson, 2001, p. 55.

13. Anthony, "Why You Should Never Center Align Paragraph Text," UX Movement, January 19, 2011. uxmovement.com/content/why-you-should-never-center-align-paragraph-text/.

14. Philip B. Meggs and Alston W. Purvis, *Meggs' History of Graphic Design*. Hoboken, NJ: John Wiley & Sons, Inc., 2012, pp. 337–338.

15. Meggs and Purvis, *Meggs' History of Graphic Design*, p. 338.

16. Robert Bieselin, "A Vague, Illustrated History of Modern Book Design in 19 Covers (and 7-10 Taco References)," Lit Reactor, May 14, 2014. litreactor.com/columns/a-vague-illustrated-history-of-modern-book-design-in-19-covers-and-7-10-taco-references.

Chapter Three: Posters for Decoration and Persuasion

17. Alois Senefelder, "The Invention of Lithography," University of Georgia Libraries, March 15, 2006. fax.libs.uga.edu/NE2420xS475/1f/invention_of_lithography.txt.

18. Philip B. Meggs, *A History of Graphic Design*. New York, NY: Wiley, 1998, p. 185.

19. Meggs, *A History of Graphic Design*, p. 183.

20. Quoted in Meggs, *A History of Graphic Design*, p. 251.

21. Quoted in Arthur Ward, *A Guide to War Publications of the First & Second World War: From Training Guides to Propaganda Posters*. South Yorkshire, UK: Pen and Sword Military, 2014, p. 26.

22. Northwestern University Library, "The World War II Poster Collection." www.library.northwestern.edu/govinfo/collections/wwii-posters/background.html.

23. Quoted in National Archives, "Powers of Persuasion." www.archives.gov/exhibits/powers_of_persuasion/its_a_womans_war_too/its_a_womans_war_too.html.

24. Quoted in Joel Selvin, "Alton Kelley, Psychedelic Poster Creator, Dies," *San Francisco Chronicle*, June 3, 2008. www.sfgate.com/cgi-bin/article.cgi?f=/c/a/2008/06/03/BAQS111UJ4.DTL.

25. Meggs, *A History of Graphic Design*, p. 404.

26. Quoted in Paul Hiebert, "What Is Punk? 25 Definitions from People Who Should Know," Flavorwire, June 21, 2010. flavorwire.com/99393/what-is-punk-25-definitions-from-people-who-should-know.

27. Quoted in Elizabeth Flock, "Why Shepard Fairey's Inauguration Protest Posters

Won't Have Trump on Them," PBS *Newshour*, last updated January 16, 2017. www.pbs.org/newshour/art/shepard-fairey-launches-people-poster-campaign-trumps-inauguration/.

Chapter Four: Design in Advertising

28. Rebecca Gross, "50 Genius Print Ads with Brilliant Design Techniques," Canva, September 9, 2015. designschool.canva.com/blog/print-advertising-ideas/.

29. Quoted in Ellen Mazur Thomson, *The Origins of Graphic Design in America, 1870–1920.* New Haven, CT: Yale University Press, 1997, p. 82.

30. Sammye Johnson and Patricia Prijatel, *The Magazine from Cover to Cover.* New York, NY: Oxford University Press, 2007, p. 79.

31. Quoted in David Crowley and Mitchell Beazley, *Magazine Covers.* London, UK: Octopus, 2006, p. 57.

32. Quoted in "1980 Hall of Fame," The Art Directors Club. www.adcglobal.org/archive/hof/1980/?id=262.

33. Steven Heller, "Gene Federico, 81, Graphic Designer, Dies," *New York Times*, September 10, 1999. www.nytimes.com/1999/09/10/business/gene-federico-81-graphic-designer-dies.html.

34. Quoted in "William Bernbach," The Advertising Century. adage.com/article/special-report-the-advertising-century/william-bernbach/140180/.

35. Josie Feliz, "The Partnership for Drug-Free Kids Unveils New Multimedia Youth Campaign Using Emojis to Let Teens Know #WeGotYou," Partnership for Drug-Free Kids, July 7, 2015. www.drugfree.org/newsroom/partnership-drug-free-kids-unveils-new-multimedia-youth-campaign-using-emojis-let-teens-know-wegotyou/.

36. Lizzie Davey, "The History and Evolution of Advertising," Tint, June 29, 2016. www.tintup.com/blog/history-evolution-advertising-marketing/.

37. Quoted in Andrew C. Revkin, "A Fresh Advertising Pitch: Buy Nothing," *New York Times*, November 22, 2007. dotearth.blogs.nytimes.com/2007/11/22/a-fresh-advertising-pitch-buy-nothing.

38. Molly Soat, "Why Print Matters," American Marketing Association, April 2015. www.ama.org/publications/MarketingNews/Pages/why-print-matters.aspx.

Chapter Five: Modern Design

39. R. Roger Remington, *American Modernism: Graphic Design, 1920–1960*. New Haven, CT: Yale University Press, 2003, p. 169.
40. Hollis, *Graphic Design*, p. 188.
41. Hollis, *Graphic Design*, p. 191.
42. Quoted in "About," Susan Kare Graphic Design. kare.com/about/.
43. "April Greiman," American Institute of Graphic Arts. www.aiga.org/content.cfm/medalist-aprilgreiman.
44. Quoted in "April Greiman," American Institute of Graphic Arts.
45. "April Greiman," American Institute of Graphic Arts.
46. Quoted in Lewis Blackwell and David Carson, *The End of Print: The Graphic Design of David Carson*. San Francisco, CA: Chronicle, 1995, p. 7.
47. Quoted in Rhonda Rubinstein, "Emigre Fonts: Interview with Zuzana Licko," *Eye*, 2002. www.emigre.com/Licko1.php.
48. Steven Heller and Seymour Chwast, *Graphic Style: From Victorian to Digital*. New York, NY: Abrams, 2000, p. 235.
49. Heller and Chwast, *Graphic Style: From Victorian to Digital*, p. 244.
50. Rachel Carlson, "The Evolution of Web Design: 1990-Present," Design Juices. www.designjuices.co.uk/2011/09/web-design-evolution/.
51. Suzanne Labarre, "The Most Important Design Jobs of the Future," *Fast Company*, January 4, 2016. www.fastcodesign.com/3054433/design-moves/the-most-important-design-jobs-of-the-future.

For More Information

Books

Blanchard, Tamsin. *Fashion and Graphics*. London, UK: Laurence King, 2004.
   This book explores the packaging that makes fashion sell, putting the spotlight on the graphic designers who mold brand images from labels to shopping bags.

Greek, Joe. *A Career in Computer Graphics and Design*. New York, NY: Rosen Publishing, 2015.
   Students who are interested in a career in graphic design learn about the types of classes and activities they can sign up for in order to get experience.

Kidd, Chip. *Go: A Kidd's Guide to Graphic Design*. New York, NY: Workman Publishing Company, Inc., 2013.
   Designer Chip Kidd introduces young adults to the basic principles of graphic design. Several design projects are included to give readers hands-on experience.

Meggs, Philip B., and Alston W. Purvis. *Meggs' History of Graphic Design*. Hoboken, NJ: John Wiley & Sons, Inc., 2012.
   This definitive history of graphic communication has vivid illustrations that chronicle the fascinating quest to give visual form to ideas.

Pease, Pamela. *Graphic Design for Kids*. Chapel Hill, NC: Paintbox Press, 2010.
   A beginner's guide to graphic design, this book discusses topics such as creativity, portfolios, the design process, and more.

Websites

AIGA

www.aiga.org

> The website of AIGA, the professional association for design, contains articles about influential designers and new developments in the field, as well as a presentation called "100 Years of Design."

DaFont

www.dafont.com

> This website offers hundreds of fonts that are free for personal use. Always ask an adult before downloading anything from the Internet.

The Father of Industrial Design: Raymond Loewy

www.raymondloewy.com

> This website is maintained to honor the life, legend, and career of product designer Raymond Loewy and includes quotes, photos, awards, and career highlights.

The Mucha Foundation

www.muchafoundation.org/home

> This website features the artwork and biography of the world-famous graphic designer Alphonse Mucha.

Nuremberg Chronicle, Beloit College

www.beloit.edu/nuremberg/index.htm

> This website contains extensive information about the layout, design, and history of the famous 15th-century block book, along with photos of hundreds of its pages.

Index

Picture Credits

Cover (screen image), cover (main image) Rawpixel.com/Shutterstock.com; pp. 1, 3–4, 6, 8, 24, 44, 66, 82, 98, 102, 104, 111–112 Lunarus/Shutterstock.com; p. 9 antishock/Shutterstock.com; p. 11 Neil Lang/Shutterstock.com; pp. 12–13 VDex/Shutterstock.com; p. 13 (inset) YamabikaY/Shutterstock.com; pp. 13, 15, 22, 27, 33, 35, 42, 47, 49, 51, 55, 58, 62, 64, 68, 74, 81, 94 (paint background) Jaroslav Machacek/Shutterstock.com; pp. 14–15 meunierd/Shutterstock.com; p. 19 Steve Dykes/Getty Images; p. 22 Shawshots/Alamy Stock Photo; p. 25 Sasha_Ivv/Shutterstock.com; pp. 26–27 CARL COURT/AFP/Getty Images; p. 30 I. Pilon/Shutterstock.com; pp. 32–33 © istockphoto.com/ferrantraite; p. 35 (top) Ajay Shrivastava/Shutterstock.com; pp. 35 (bottom), 57, 58 courtesy of the Library of Congress; p. 40 Robert Estall photo agency/Alamy Stock Photo; p. 42 (top) CHANCE YEH /Patrick McMullan via Getty Images; p. 42 (bottom) Yann Gamblin/Paris Match via Getty Images; p. 45 © istockphoto.com/ valentinrussanov; p. 47 Swim Ink 2, LLC/CORBIS/Corbis via Getty Images; p. 49 from The New York Public Library; p. 51 (top) EQRoy/Shutterstock.com; p. 51 (bottom) standa_art/Shutterstock.com; p. 54 (left) Everett Historical/ Shutterstock.com; p. 54 (right) 'I Want Out'/Private Collection/Peter Newark American Pictures/Bridgeman Images; p. 55 MatiasDelCarmine/ Shutterstock.com; p. 62 Michael Ochs Archives/Getty Images; pp. 64–65 AP Photo/Damian Dovarganes; p. 68 Julie Clopper/Shutterstock.com; p. 70 charles whitefield/Shutterstock.com; pp. 74–75 Benoit Daoust/Shutterstock.com; pp. 80–81 © istockphoto.com/Anna Bryukhanova; p. 85 © Susan Kare Graphic Design; p. 88 alexander kirch/iStockphoto.com; p. 92 © Emigre Inc.; pp. 94–95 Georgejmclittle/Shutterstock.com; back cover vector illustration/ Shutterstock.com.

About the Author

Donna Reynolds is a freelance writer and editor who has worked on more than 50 books for young adults. She has a degree in English from the University of Wisconsin–Madison and spends as much time as possible traveling around the world. She tries to volunteer at a local nonprofit organization at least one day a week, wherever she happens to be.